A Mystics Journey

A Life of Encounter

By
BRACY WEVERS

A Catalyst for Transformation

Published by Seraph Creative in 2025

United States / United Kingdom / South Africa / Australia

www.seraphcreative.org

ISBN 978-1-964959-82-5 (hardcover)

ISBN 978-1-964959-61-0 (paperback)

eBook 978-1-964959-60-3

From Jenny Pizot, High School World Language teacher and 1st editor of the book

A compelling and heart-wrenching account of a spiritual journey, which results in a transformed lifestyle. Bracy makes a soul-searching journey and leaves the reader to find the same answers to questions about leading a fulfilled life. I highly recommend 'A Mystics Journey-A life of Encounter' as a divine gift for anyone who is inquisitive. Bracy's book ultimately points us to a more profound understanding of God and our destiny on this earth.

Dedication

This book is dedicated to:

First and foremost, to my Heavenly Father, Abba, Yahweh.
To Yeshua.
To Ruach HaKodesh.
My love, my breath, my protector, my strong tower.
Sustainer, creator, upholder of all things, you're guidance is perfect.

To Wisdom, in all her splendor, for being who you are and loving me.

To the 7 spirits of God, for teaching, training and equipping me.

To all the ones surrounding my life.
The canopy of angels.
The heavenly beings.
My cloud of witnesses.
For helping me, supporting me and cheering me on.

To my Mom and my grandma, Nanny, who I never knew.
And to all the generations who have loved the Lord and the blessings
Passed down to me through them.
I am eternally grateful.

FOREWORD

When someone you care about invites you into the story of their spiritual journey, you're not just reading words on a page—you're walking beside them through moments of transformation, doubt, clarity, and grace. That's what this book offers: not a map, but a lantern. It lights the way not with answers, but with honest reflections, personal revelations, and the quiet strength that comes from walking an authentic path.

I've had the privilege of knowing Bracy (Sarai) Wevers not just as a friend, but as a fellow seeker. Over the years, I've watched her wrestle with the big questions—Who am I? Why am I here? Where is the Divine in all of this?—with humility, courage, and a depth of heart that is rare and beautiful. What you'll find in these pages is a testament to that journey.

This is not a book of spiritual clichés or quick fixes. It's a deeply human account of awakening—told with honesty, vulnerability, and at times, breathtaking insight. Whether you are on your own spiritual path, feeling lost, or simply curious, this book meets you where you are and gently invites you to further reflect on your spiritual journey.

Jenny Pizot, friend and fellow seeker

Table of Contents

MYSTIC

(mis-tik) noun

Someone who believes in unseen realities. One who believes that they can have access to hidden mysteries, transcending ordinary human knowledge. One who believes they can know God.

Did you know that if you live and move in the spirit, you are a mystic? If you comprehend truths not conceived by the intellect, you are a mystic. It's not an intellectual state, it's a spiritual home (Kathy Walters)

Dictionary.com: *noun* - a person who claims to attain, or believes in the possibility of attaining, insight into mysteries transcending ordinary human knowledge, as any direct communication with the divine or immediate intuition in a state of spiritual ecstasy.

Oxford dictionary: A person who seeks by contemplation and self-surrender to obtain unity with or absorption into the Deity or the absolute, or who believes in the spiritual apprehension of truths that are beyond the intellect.

Wikipedia: Deriving from Neo-Platonism and Henosis, mysticism is popularly known as union with God or the Absolute. In the 13th century, the term *unio mystica* came to be used to refer to the "spiritual marriage," the ecstasy, or rapture, that was experienced when prayer was used "to contemplate both God's omnipresence in the world and God in his essence." In the 19th century, under the influence of Romanticism, this "union" was interpreted as a "religious experience," which provides certainty about God or a transcendental reality.

INTRODUCTION

I had a dream the other night about writing a book about my supernatural experiences and encounters with God. I could see it so clearly, all lined out.

Having started four books already and having 'the goal' to write for twenty years, I started this project early in 2019, declaring that I would finish this one. I have pressed on to finish this project, not so for me, but for you to know what the possibility is of being in God and being One with Him and the knowledge and understanding of having Him live on the inside of you and all that this entails. My belief is that all of this, all of what I have written about here, should be normal in our spiritual walk in God, should be normal everyday occurrences as Sons of God, co-creating with our heavenly Father.

My encounters started in high school, the day I gave the Lord my heart in the library of my high school in Winter Park, Florida.

I have to say that each encounter has just come. It's not something that I am seeking in the moment. It is as Holy Spirit wills. It is the way God speaks to me, shows me things, and it is how I know things. Most often, the experiences come first, and then, sometimes years later, confirmation in the word is revealed to me.

I have wanted this book to show a progression of my journey with God, starting with my encounters before I knew the Lord and continuing through as the Lord matured me. The early encounters are significant, but they were tempered by the Lord to not overwhelm me too much. As I grew in maturity in Him, He could give me more and more revelation and I hope this journey shows that.

I believe that we must be taught by the Lord in all things, supernatural things, no longer relying on a man in a pulpit, or a speaker and their own personal revelations. The Lord wants to teach us individually. Sure, speakers and preachers and others will come along to confirm what God is saying, but you must be taught by Him and no one else. Revelation must come from Him first and not a person.

Yahweh – YHVH - (the Hebrew word for God) is so vast and multidimensional that we will never be able to comprehend the richness of His majesty. All our different puzzle pieces fit together like a tapestry woven together through love. That is what binds us together in Unity.

Unity loves diversity. Unity loves the many different parts of all of us put together. We are Living Stones put together as a living tapestry. That is why we must honor one another and love each other's giftings because we all fit together as ONE.

The Echad – oneness - unity in diversity. Echad is the Hebrew word for one. The correct concept of our God is the word Echad. It means a single entity but made up of more than one part. (Kehilanews)

Deuteronomy 6:4 – Hear O Israel, YHVH our God is ONE (Echad)

This, unity-loving diversity, gives us the freedom for you to be you and me to be me. We fit together like living stones that cannot be broken. There is no need for competition. We all fit together.

I want to say this again because it is so important - All the prophetic words that I have received in my journey have been spoken to my heart from the Lord FIRST. Not spoken to me by a man.

Let me reiterate ... not by a man but by the Lord!

He is the one who has prophesied TO me and then confirmed it through other people or circumstances, so that I know it is Him speaking to me. He has taught me to hear His voice.

We are forever learning and growing, coming into the journey of bringing us into our identity of who we really are! We need to embrace that process, which will bring greater responsibility and rulership. True Sons do the things that Jesus showed us. This is the key. Re-establishing dominion and bringing things back to their original intent, back to the original design that God had in His heart before He created.

Wisdom needs to be incorporated in our everyday life and the seven spirits of God should be our tutors. The angels are awaiting our declarations so they can carry out their assignments on the earth. Decrees are designed to transform the earth. We need to train our senses to engage the angelic realm, the heavenly realms of His Glory.

(Wisdom - study and meditate about Wisdom in Proverbs 2)

The last couple of decades should have been the FIVE-FOLD teaching us all these things, but people were busy building their own platforms. We have much to learn. We have passed out of the FIVE-FOLD and into Sonship, ruling as Kings and Priests unto our God and co-creating with Christ.

One thing that you must know about me is my naivete and curiosity. These two things have been the underlying factors that have led me into most of my encounters. Holy Spirit grabs my curiosity and takes me on a journey, as I follow Him into the depths unknown.

Each chapter in this book is a different experience in the Lord. I have tried to choose the ones Holy Spirit is highlighting me to tell, as there have been many in my life. I have tried to choose the most important ones, the significant ones that brought transformation, revelation or a knowing. Holy Spirit wills us to know Him more and through experience and encounter, we can come to a deeper revelation of who He is and who we are in Christ. I have to say that everything, every encounter, visitation, and experience has been confirmed in the Word of God.

My hope for this endeavor is for you to be brought to a spiritual hunger for more, to know Him in a deeper way, to experience God like you never have before and to excite you in the supernatural ways of the Spiritual realms.

Thank you for taking the time to read this testimony of His Glorious and Supernatural ways. This is my journey of learning how to hear His voice and to be obedient to what He says, to know of His goodness and mercy and that He is faithful to the end. I pray you will be taken up in the Spirit and encounter Him. I hope you enjoy my journey.

FOOTNOTE:

FIVE-FOLD ministry:

Apostles – Prophets – Evangelists – Pastors - Teachers

And he gave some with grace to be apostles; and some with grace to be prophets; and some with grace to be evangelists; and some with grace to be pastors and some with grace to be teachers; and their calling is to nurture and prepare all the holy believers to do their own works of ministry, and as they do this they will enlarge and build up the body of Christ. These grace ministries will function until we all attain oneness in the faith, until we all experience the fullness of what it means to know the Son of God, and finally we become one perfect man with full dimensions of spiritual maturity and fully developed in the abundance of Christ. (The Passion translation)

Seven Spirits of God:

*Isaiah 11:1 ... A shoot will come out from the stump of Jesse, and a branch will bear fruit from his roots. The **Spirit of the Lord** will rest upon him, the **Spirit of wisdom** and **understanding**, the **Spirit of counsel** and **might**, the **Spirit of knowledge** and **fear of the Lord**. (International Standard version)*

Revelation 1:4 ... From John to the seven churches in western Turkey: may the kindness of God's grace and peace overflow to you from him who is, and who was, and who is to come, and from the seven spirits who are in front of his throne, and from Jesus Christ the faithful witness, the firstborn from the dead and the ruling Kings, who rules of the kings of the earth!

The purpose of the Seven Spirits of God is to teach us, train us and equip us in the mysteries of God, as there are many, many realms to explore; to empower us to be Kings and Priests and heirs of God and all that entails; to open up and show us how to live from an ascended place in the heavenly realms, swirling in the whirlwind of His mysteries, becoming who we were created to be.

The Spirit of the Lord – color red – equips us for positional dominion and teaches us God's divine order and alignment of His government and His glory.

Spirit of Wisdom – color orange – equips us for position. It teaches us how to bring divine order and authority out of the throne as Sons into the spiritual realm, bringing divine justice, and to bring authority and dominion and divine order to the earth.

Spirit of Understanding – color green – helps us to use what we have at the right time, to decipher revelation, encounters, and visions, how to perceive the realms of the Kingdom and how to rule as Sons.

Spirit of Counsel – color yellow – teaches us how to access the counsels of God, how to commune with Him and understand His advice, how to resolve issues and bring Godly advice.

Spirit of Knowledge – color blue – teaches us how to access the knowledge of God and how to apply it, helps to gain knowledge about the supernatural realms of God.

Spirit of Might – color indigo – teaches us about our strength as Sons and our absolute dominion, teaches us how to understand and reveal the power of God.

Spirit of the Fear of the Lord – color violet – the fear is not one of being afraid but of understanding God's great and vast majesty and awe and dominion, teaches us about the realms of holiness and intimacy and worship.

PART ONE

My name IS my personality

My full name is Sarah Bracy, but people call me Bracy. My mother's name was Sarah, and my parents didn't want me to be called Little Sarah, so they called me by my middle name, Bracy. It is a family name and part of my heritage. My great Aunt Sue was the last of the Bracys. Some of my kinfolk back east in the South still call me by my full name, Sarah Bracy.

The name BRACY is French in origin. It was quite an encounter to find out that my name is French in origin. My parents had passed away already, and I think they would've been shocked to find this out. All my life, I thought my name was of British origin.

My Alabama French friend who lives near Paris, who is an expert at researching things, found this meaning of the name Bracy. I was sitting at my desk one day while living in Paris and I got the email from my friend. I opened the email and to my complete surprise, my eyes fell on this first:

BRACY .... (Origin French) Locality. From Bracy (Brecey), a town in Normandy.

You are an inspiring leader whose originality, creativity and wisdom are applied to creating practical solutions to 'unsolvable' problems. Humanitarian and idealistic your vision is to make the world a better place and you will work to this end. Hardworking and tenacious people admire you for your honesty and integrity. You are a loved and loyal friend and partner. You have the potential to achieve enormous success in the world.

I sat at my desk, stunned. I had to pause for a minute and read it again. French? What?

In a flash of an instant, my complete identity changed. Growing up, we all knew the family name Bracy was British. There was never a mention of it being French. Ever.

I sat stunned at my desk for a long while trying to understand what was being revealed to me at this moment, because it was a big moment. I could feel its significance.

At that time, I was asking Abba – why did you bring a French man into my life to marry?

.. and then this pops up.

So, my name … my ACTUAL NAME that my parents gave me AT birth … is French and there is a town in Normandy, where my husband grew up, WITH MY NAME ON IT!

The revelation hit me hard, like a solid foundation settling into the ground.

Yahweh changed the whole conversation in my head about my husband and answered the question of whether we were meant to be together. This settled that conversation. How can you argue with your name branded in your DNA and it being a place where your husband grew up? Case settled.

Most of my life, I have ignored the Sarah part of my name. I viewed it as a hindrance and annoyingly, at school, I would have to point out that my name was Bracy and not Sarah. I used to sit in the Doctor's office waiting room and they would call out my name – Sarah? – Sarah? - Sarah Wevers? It took me a while to get used to using my first name after all the privacy laws. Now they must use your whole name.

I never identified with Sarah. I felt almost as if I should change my name and get rid of it, but when I changed my name when I got married 38 years ago, I dropped my last name and kept Sarah. The meaning of Sarah is Princess.

People know me by my name, Bracy. They think I am strong and bold, kind of a bulldozer, hanging on like a dog on a bone with things I set out to do. It must be the way I appear, because I have had this spoken over me many times, saying how strong I am. I always accepted this, thinking this is what it looks like to press through great challenges in weakness, because this is what I was doing. Obedience to the Lord might sometimes look like boldness and courage to others. I am just following His lead.

I was at a conference in Coeur D'Alene, Idaho, in 2013 and in a time of worship, Yahweh renamed me.

He said, 'I am moving you from Bracy to Sarah. This is your new name now'.

My sight was opened, and I could see how He was moving me from 'brace yourself for Bracy' to 'sweet tenderhearted Sarah'. I could see that in the spirit.

I haven't changed my name to Sarah. I haven't had people start calling me Sarah. I don't know why. It feels weird. I like being called Bracy.

I've been dealing with some stuff from my past and I was talking with an awesome friend who really does 'see' me rightly.

She said, 'Oh yes, people see the outside of you, strong, bold, but you only let a few in so far that can see the 'tender heart' that you are'.

I started crying, and I knew she was right. I'm going to try harder to let that tenderhearted Sarah part of me come out and shine.

So, all that to say... My name is my personality. Is it yours too?

Ask Yahweh about your name.

Get quiet with Him somewhere you will not be distracted and ask the Lord about your name. Have a pen and paper ready so that you can write down all that He will reveal to you about your name and what it means.

The day I opened my heart

It's funny how I can't remember what I did last week, but I can remember my encounters with God so clearly. It is like they are living and real. The clarity comes when I think back on them and I am able to relive them again and again, knowing His faithfulness surrounds me.

I believe I was around 16 when this first encounter happened. I love the theater and was part of a Christian Thespian group in high school. An itinerant minister named Pat had been invited to come and speak. We all met in the library. I remember the room being very full and I was sitting cross-legged on top of a table off to the side.

I don't remember anything that Pat said, but I do remember being riveted and focused on what he was saying. So much so that when he led us into a prayer, my heart and soul were all in.

Pat led us in the prayer where you visualize and imagine your own heart. There is a throne there in the middle of it and you are seated on that throne, meaning you are in control of your life.

The prayer takes you through a visualization of imagining yourself on the throne and seeing Jesus standing beside you, while you are seated on your throne.

Then Pat asked us to stand up and come off our throne and ask Jesus to come and sit down on the throne and take His place in the center of our hearts.

As I said the prayer along with everyone in the library that day, I was supernaturally lifted up above everyone in that library into a cloud-like presence. I felt like I was being lifted off the ground into the heavens, into the spirit. The atmosphere was a wonderful, warm feeling, filled with a peace I had never experienced before. I was saturated with a warmth and a goodness that you could taste.

It was incredible.

(If you do not know Jesus or His great love for you, ask Jesus to come and take His place on the throne of your heart. It is as simple as that. I pray that when you do that you would be surrounded by His Joy, and Peace and have a great understanding of His love for you.)

Pray – Jesus, come and take your place on the throne of my heart. I surrender my life to you.

Commissioned for worship

Around the same time frame when I got saved in the library of my high school, I had another important encounter. In fact, this encounter still sits with me to this day, as I have not seen its fulfillment.

At this time in my life, I was feeling a very strong pull to sing, dance and perform. Ever since I was a little girl, I would pretend to be on stage in front of millions of people and sing along into my hairbrush with my favorite albums, Elton John, James Taylor, and George Harrison, playing on my pink record player. My first solo in church was when I was in the sixth grade.

As a junior in high school, I attended First Presbyterian church in Orlando, Florida. At church, we were doing a musical in the spring called 'Light Shine'. I auditioned and won the big solo in the middle of the program.

We had weeks of rehearsal, and I was very excited and very nervous.

This was a big thing for my church. The night of the performance was a big night, complete with a whole church potluck dinner.

I remember being so nervous.

The musical starts, and everything is going well. I thought we were all doing a great job.

I got up to take my place to sing the big climatic solo and the moment I stood up, I was flooded, all around me, with this warmth, like being covered in a cloud of honey. It felt like liquid love was surrounding me in a bubble. I looked down in front of me and this elderly gentleman was looking up at me, right at me, staring at me. His eyes were fixed on me. He was wrapped up in the atmosphere, too. I could feel his delight in me and what I was singing. He smiled at me and he seemed to be glowing. In fact, the bubble was glowing. I can remember it so clearly, even now, after all these years. I was singing and it felt like I was glowing. Everything was golden and warm and electrifying.

In the midst of this glowing bubble, I heard a voice say ... 'I have called you as a Christian singer'.

At the time, there weren't any Christian singers, no worship groups or singers, not like today.

I remember thinking... What is that?

Instantly, I had a vision of a man that was sitting at a keyboard and he was watching me sing, and I KNEW he was approving of me and what I was doing. It was like he was coaching me. I felt like he would be instrumental in my growth as a Christian singer, whatever that meant.

I have never felt so loved and encouraged in that moment. I had no idea what it meant.

The Lord led me to study music at Pacific Lutheran University, PLU, specializing in vocal performance. At the time, it didn't make sense, but as I look back on my life, I get it now.

He was guiding me, leading me and I didn't know it.

One year, during a Christmas concert that we did with my university, PLU, as we were singing, Holy Spirit came upon me so strongly that I started crying while we were singing. The conductor just looked at me with compassionate eyes, trying to make sure I was ok, but I could feel God's presence so strongly. It was so beautiful and pure and warm and amazing. All I could do was cry at its beauty.

(Someone suggested that this might have been an angel, this man at the keyboard. If this is true, and it was an angel and not an actual person, this changes everything. This is something for me to go back and ask the Lord about after all these years. Maybe this angel has been with me all my life since that time and I didn't know it. I am excited to find out.

Sometimes the Lord gives us something and we think it is in the natural and we think we know what it looks like. When in fact, it is something entirely different.

For example - when we lived in Paris from 2001-2005, the Lord told me I was going to plant a Vineyard. I took that to mean that I was going to actually plant a Vineyard church in Paris. Seems silly now, but I took it seriously and really set out to do just that. I wasted a lot of effort pursuing this interpretation.

We were in the car taking our exit home in the States after moving back, and the Lord showed me the vineyard of unity that I/we had planted in Paris. Beautiful rows of a well-watered planted vineyard were what I saw. I wept and laughed at His marvelous, amazing ways that He accomplishes things despite us.)

Driving while considering Faust

The first time the enemy tried to kill me, I was driving a brand-new Mercedes 320 that my Dad had on loan for a couple of days from his friend Joe to see if he wanted to buy it. Daddy collected Mercedes and restored them back to their original interior, complete with the original walnut dashboard and leather seats. He had four collectibles at home that he was working on. I used to sneak the car keys out of his top dresser drawer and take the hardtop 230 convertible for a spin, always remembering to put the keys back in the exact place and position I had found them. A couple of times, I had a near miss. It is funny how careless we are when we are young and free.

The previous week, Joe had offered me a job driving luxury cars (Jags, Porsches, and Mercedes) from Jacksonville to Orlando. I was elated at the prospect. I persuaded Daddy to let me take the new car on loan to my dance class. I was sixteen, a sophomore in high school, an honor student and very responsible. Daddy said, "yes".

The scene was straight out of a movie. Steven Spielberg could not have set the scene up better. We were studying Faust in English class and I was intensely absorbed in the tension between God and the devil over Faust's soul. In the story, the devil makes a pact with God, which says, if he (Faust) ever says, 'Let this moment last forever, Faust is mine'.

(Faust (Part One) is a complex story. It takes place in multiple settings, the first of which is <u>heaven</u>. Mephistopheles makes a bet with God: he says that he can defect God's favorite human being (Faust), who is striving to learn everything that can be known, away from righteous pursuits.) (Wikipedia, the Free Encyclopedia, Wikipedia Foundation)

This story touched something deep inside me. An itinerant minister had come, just months beforehand, to preach at my high school to the Thespians, a Christian theater club that I was involved in. This day was the day I opened my heart to Yeshua. Overcome with what the minister was saying, I said the prayer along with him, visually focusing on the picture in my hands of two thrones.

On one throne sat a person. This was supposed to be me, showing how I was at the center of my life, in charge of all that I do and the decisions that I make. The other throne had a heart. Yeshua sat in the middle of it. Sitting there and focusing on putting Yeshua in the middle of my heart, I felt like I was supernaturally lifted up above everyone, off the ground in the spirit into this wonderful, atmospheric cloud, filled with peace, warmth and goodness that I had never known or felt before.

With my recent encounter and Faust weighing heavy on my mind, I got in the car to go to dance class. Driving along in this amazing car, feeling unbelievable, I felt the richness of the car, the music on the radio, and the smoothness of the ride. Life looked good. Life felt good.

Something started to pull me into a strange, euphoric state, potent and intense. It was as if the entire pull of the passions and desires of the world were intensifying and pulling me towards them. The Faust story was coming to life right there in my world. Alluring, it was filled with lustful desires of power and riches and money. The sensation was intensifying, and the car was filled with this worldly sensual feeling. I gave way to it, knowing deep down that it was a dangerous place, knowing that I shouldn't, but I was unable to resist the pull.

I said to myself, under my breath in a whisper, 'Oh, if only this moment could last a little longer'.

The minute the words came out of my mouth, I regretted it. I knew I had done something wrong, feeling the effect even before anything happened. An intense implosion hit the car.

WHAM!! The impact imploded all around me, as another car rammed into the front, right side of the Mercedes.

My car had been hit at an angle and started to spin around and around.

Immediately, I was shaken out of my euphoric, trance-like state into a bad dream, spinning around and around, with no way out. I held onto the steering wheel for dear life.

As the car spun around and around, I felt a presence wrap itself around me and protect me. Physically, I sensed the warm, pillow-like softness completely surrounding me as the car continued to spin in circles into the middle of this big highway intersection.

(As I look back, I know it was my guardian angels linking hands to surround me and protect me.)

The car screeched to a standstill stop and, in a flash of an instant, I realized that I was not hurt.

Unbelievable! Something had saved me and protected me from harm! I pushed the car door open with force, jumped out of the car and fell to the ground on all fours. I started pounding the highway pavement with my fist, screaming, "Look at what you have done! You idiot!! Are you kidding me? Ahhhhhh!!! I can't believe this!!!"

A man driving a red Dodge Dart had run a red light and slammed into me. I walked out of the accident totally unscathed, no wounds or hurts, not even a cut or bruise.

The Mercedes I was driving was totally crushed on both ends of the car, front and back. I couldn't believe I had nothing on me: no cuts, no wounds, not even a bruise. It was a miracle! I knew I had been rescued by angels of the Lord!

Joe, the owner of the dealership where my dad had borrowed the car and who had just hired me the week before to drive luxury cars down from Jacksonville to Orlando, showed up on the accident scene and said, 'Well, Bracy, honey, about the job, I don't think it's going work out.'

We had a long laugh about that.

My Deliverance Story

Sometimes I think that you have to be lied to to get you in the exact place that God wants you. Or at least I did. That is exactly what my good friend did. She lied to me.

So, we are in the year 2000.

I was having trouble with my middle daughter. She was crying all the time, and I wasn't sure what to do or even why she was crying so much. I mentioned this to my friend, and she said she was going to this parenting group and that it might help me.

(Of course, this was not a parenting group, but a small women's group out of the Vancouver Vineyard church. I didn't know this. I came for the childcare.)

Looking back, I realize that God placed me in this beautiful, warm and loving cocoon with some mature Christian women, who loved me and led me, as Holy Spirit inundated me with encounter after encounter. It was a fast, steep learning curve that year in Holy Spirit School, and I was learning so much. I still have the prophetic words that they all spoke over me.

One Monday morning, the women were going on and on about spiritual warfare. One woman said, 'If you don't know it is all about spiritual warfare, you are not on the bus'.

Obviously, I was not on the bus and had no idea what she was talking about. It sounded like Chinese to me. Not knowing at all what she was talking about, I raised my hand and asked some questions.

One lady said, you need to go to Emmanuel bookstore and buy a book on spiritual warfare. So, I went to the bookstore. It was local, just down the street from my house.

It was interesting because I was starting to feel a divine hand on my being there.

Perusing the aisles and carrying some books around in my hands, the owner of the bookstore came up to me and asked me if I needed any help. I explained what I was looking for.

She said, 'Oh, you have to buy this book! This is the book you want. This is the book for you! It helped me so much! You don't want those other books. They're good – but not like this one!' She shoved a pink-colored book into my hands.

She was so insistent. I felt like I couldn't leave the store without buying the book. She forced me to buy Frank and Shirley Solberg's book on spiritual warfare.

I took the book home and started to read it. The beginning grabbed me immediately. I was in a Lutheran church at the time and in the introduction of the book, the author tells the story of how he started his ministry in a Lutheran church. Holy Spirit was leading me, guiding me and confirming that I was to continue to read this book.

I was hooked. There were many hooks like this, intriguing, moving me to finish the book.

(The title of the Book is A Time for WAR: Spiritual Battle Strategies for the Christian by Pastor Frank Solberg)

As I finished the book, I had the thought that it would be nice one day to check out and see what was in my basement, so to speak. One day in the future, mind you.

Sitting on my couch and reflecting on what I had read, I took the book in my hands and started looking through the book. I never do this. Once I am done reading something, I put it away and that's it. But I kept looking. I opened to the front page and right there on the inside cover was information about Frank and Shirley and their address. I looked up the address and realized it was five minutes from my house!

I sat there for a minute to think about this huge coincidence.

I started saying things out loud like: 'Oh no Lord, I don't want to do that now. I meant in the future', 'that's not what I meant'.

I started to wrestle with the Lord, feeling not ready for what He was leading me into. Fear of the unknown was prevalent, but I was starting to learn that His Leadership is perfect and that He is for me and will not lead me astray. I can trust Him. He is faithful.

I looked in the phone book for Frank's number. I found it and left the phone book open on the table for a week contemplating, and then one morning I gathered up enough courage and called the number.

The phone conversation went like this:

Frank - 'Hello'

Me - 'Hello Mr. Solberg'

Frank – 'Why are you calling?'

Me – 'I don't know. I just read your book and I feel like I need to see you'

Frank – 'Come Thursday, 10:00 am fasting'

Me – 'Ok'

I hung up and was flooded with … What have I done?

From my journal, May 2nd, 2001...

I made this appointment 1 ½ weeks ago because I had read Frank's book and I felt a need to see someone like this, but I thought it would never happen ... until I found out that they lived 5 minutes away from my house!!

I fasted and showed up at their house. I wasn't scared at all. I had no idea what this was all about. I had a strange peace about me.

Frank and Shirley met me at the door and took me downstairs. The minute we got downstairs, Shirley asked me if I was rebellious. I said maybe. They both asked me some questions. We talked about my faith and all the things that had happened to me so far. I told them I didn't believe people could be slain in the spirit, that they were faking it. Shirley then proceeded to tell me the number of times it had happened to her. I was skeptical about that.

From my journal...

I arrived a little early, went to the bathroom and then went downstairs with both Frank and Shirley. Frank sat in front of me, across the table from me. Shirley sat off to the right of me. We talked for a while. He asked me questions about the book, if I had any questions for him. He asked me if I understood the body, soul, spirit concept, where the spirit can be filled with the Holy Spirit, but the soul is full of demons in the fleshly body. I said yes, I understood this.

He asked about my spiritual life. I said I was on fire for God. I told him about Weigh Down and the prophetic intercessory morning group I was in. I told him about our moving to France and how the Lord had orchestrated the whole move.

He asked more questions. I told him something about my grandmother and my problem with my weight. He was sitting at a table across from me and Shirley was to my right. Frank told me he had the gift of knowledge and Shirley had the gift of discernment. I had no idea what he meant by that.

Frank started praying prayers of protection over the house, the property, over both of them, over me, my family and friends. He covered everything.

Then, he broke off all communication and contact with Satan and principalities outside the protective barrier of the house. He cut off communication and contact with the demons, spirits, and me. This was so the spirits wouldn't be able to communicate or have any access to influence me or what was going on. He broke all communication between the spirits inside and bound them in heaven and on earth. He bound all violence and any manifestations of violence.

He then asked if I was ok. I said yes ...

I have to admit at this time that I was completely at peace and had the utmost confidence that I was there on purpose.

From my journal...

Next, he prayed a confessional prayer for the sins of my forefathers and named about 50 –60 sins that could be handed down, curses through the generations. He prayed and broke the generational curses. He asked for forgiveness and acceptance of this forgiveness. Then he cast all demons out, saying they had no legal ground.

At that moment, I saw pictures of empty, hollow, white figures with their mouths open, flee and rise and come out of my body. There were maybe 4 or 5 of them.

Frank asked what happened and I told him.

He said ... hmmmm ...

I really thought at that moment that I could have done that. That I could have made that up.

Frank asked if I was ok. I said yes ...

Then he prayed off something else from my forefathers and my hands became very warm.

Next, he prayed to break the curse from my grandmother. I don't know why or what was involved with her, but the minute Frank broke this curse, I immediately started to weep intensely, to the point that instantly the top of my shirt was sopping wet with my tears.

I looked up at Frank and said, 'What was that?'

Frank asked if I was ok. I said yes ...

Frank asked if there was incest in my family. I said none that I knew of. Frank said that there had to be someone touching someone in the past 10 generations, so we will just pray it anyway.

I said ok.

He started to cast this out, and my legs started to tense up and twitch, and my feet started to move and tap the ground. They prayed off the spirit of lust, and I really started to twitch uncontrollably.

I instantly looked at Shirley, and she was reassuring. I held onto my chair, as this was being pulled out of me. The feeling was so intense. It took a while and was very strong. As it came out, they sent it to the ground and burned it.

Frank asked if I was ok. I looked at him, surprised at what had just happened and said yes ...

I looked a right mess at this point. I was crying and shaking, shocked and surprised.

This was just the beginning. Now we were moving into more discernment.

Frank started casting out whatever came. The first big one was rebellion. It was so strong, it almost pulled me out of my chair. I had to hold on to the back of my chair, it was strong.

From my journal...

Then they prayed off the spirit of rebellion and that was a struggle, as if something was being pulled from my stomach area, as if I was birthing this.

It was weird and very strong.

It was choking me and if Frank had not bound the violence, he said it would have been dangerous. I was hanging on to the back of my chair, clinging to it. My legs were shaking uncontrollably continuously. I felt my insides were in turmoil.

There were more, many more.

From my journal...

They prayed off the appetite of something and broke all ties to rebellion. Then there were 2 or 3 other violent manifestations prayed off. Frank asked them to name themselves, their legal ground that they were still claiming and their action.

One was lewdness. The praying out was violent and took quite a long time. It was being wrenched from my body. This was very difficult physically and took a lot out of me. There was also one more demon that came out willfully but was unnamed.

Each time Frank would finish, I would hear him say ... in the name of Jesus Christ. It was so loud, so powerful and so strong, booming into me like a loud, authoritative voice!

For 3 hours, they cast out some big demons and spirits. I was ravaged. Things were being ripped from me. They left open, bloody, ravaged places all in my stomach area. I could feel the places and wounds. (These were spiritual wounds, not actual wounds in the natural, but they felt like it.)

(All during this process, Frank's voice anchored me with his calm, strong, authoritative voice. I knew this was the Lord's doing and I was a willing participant.)

I looked up at Shirley and said, 'Well, I guess I believe all that spiritual stuff now!'

We all laughed.

From my journal...

Frank and Shirley both prayed off all these spirits and then Frank prayed for healing so that Holy Spirit would fill those holes which were empty now.

He said ... we are the house wreckers and now it was up to me to pray and listen to worship music to renew my soul and renew my mind. He said it was now up to me to rebuild what had been torn down by reading the word of God and listening to worship music.

After the whole three hours of deliverance prayer, my legs were still slightly twitching and tired from my muscles being tense for so long. When I spoke, my voice was so loud in my head, like the volume of my voice was too loud for me to bear. My body was spent and tired, and I felt so weird about what had just transpired. It was hard to physically leave their house. I had a hard time walking up the stairs. I couldn't believe what had just happened.

I got to my car with great difficulty. After shaking continuously for 3 hours, I was exhausted. I had a hard time going up the stairs to get out of the basement. Shirley had to walk me out, holding my arm, I was so weak and just not stable. Totally woozy and lightheaded, I sat in my car and I felt so lost. I started weeping and sobbing uncontrollably in my car. I felt the ravaged places that were ripped from me. I saw them in the spirit and they were oozing and bloody.

I had a vision of myself: I was a warrior, all clad in armor and coming back from battle. I was all bandaged up from my head to my toes and on crutches. The bandages wrapped all around my head and around my body, almost like a mummy. They were soaked in blood and oozing like fresh wounds. My insides, where my stomach is, were all covered in blood and raw, big sores.

Sitting in my car, I realized that I was a new person, a completely new person. It was such a joyous moment when I realized that I was free of all those things and thoughts that had pushed me around all my life. I became aware of what they had done. They had become part of my personality and they were gone now.

All those thoughts that had been with me my whole life and attacked me and made me do things, they were gone, and in that moment, I didn't know who I was. It was like my personality had been completely changed into a new person.

From my journal...

I had agreed to meet a close friend afterwards and she was waiting for my call. She was worried about me and I had agreed to meet with her afterwards to make sure I was ok. I tried to pull myself together, sitting in my car after I don't know how long and called her. Luckily, she was going to be late. I sat there and realized I was finally free from my thoughts. I was not hungry, even though I had fasted so far. I was free from hunger. The freedom brought me to tears, uncontrollable sobbing. I felt so weird, like I was out of my body.

I agreed to meet my friend, who was standing by curious to know what had happened, at Café Devine. I was crying my eyes out and couldn't stop. This powerful moment was lingering, and the intensity was still there. It was dangerous to drive there, but my friend said she would pray for me. I was out of it completely.

From my journal...

I met my friend at Café Devine, and I couldn't understand anything she was saying. She was talking and asking me questions and it was as if I couldn't hear her nor understand what she was saying. I explained everything to her as best as I could. She kept asking me questions, but when she would talk, I couldn't understand her. I couldn't hear her. I kept saying, 'What are you saying?' It was as if I was not there.

As I am writing this, my legs are so sore and tired, and I am finally getting back inside my body ... that's just weird! But my legs are so tired and sore, and I am exhausted, but I can't sit down.

I feel weak and fragile and need some healing for my soul and the ravaged and ripped places that the spirits damaged as they were coming out.

Come Holy spirit and heal me. I will ask every day for your healing powers to fill me up and fill the holes that were left. Thank you, Jesus, for this cleansing. I give God the Father all the praise and Glory in my life.

I realized all the lies that Satan had told me throughout the years. I have wasted so much time. I am free now.

That night, I went to bed at 8pm and awoke at 2am. I felt so lost and started crying. I didn't know who I was. I felt lost. I did not recognize myself.

I thought ... will I still be funny? I said out loud that I miss my rebellion and immediately repented and said, 'No, I don't!'

I got out of bed and went downstairs and opened my Bible and the words on the page opened up like the petals of a flower before my eyes. The words were alive. For the first time, I was understanding the hidden mysteries of the words as I was reading and thought Wow! So, this is why people read this.

Everything opened up for me and I had eyes to see and understand. As I read the New Testament in the following days, it was as if it was telling of my life experience. I was living what was written! I was changed and was never the same after.

From my journal...

5 – 03 – 01 ... I can't believe how changed I feel. I can be so silent, as if I don't ever need to speak. Who am I? Where is my spunk? Did I do the right thing? God help me find myself. I feel like my whole personality has been uprooted and changed.

Comforting thoughts are coming now. I am still who I was, but kinder, gentler, not so loud, silent. I never would've thought. That spirit of rebellion was very strong, and I feel like I miss it. Grief and sorrow. I don't want it back, though.

I am mourning the death of me.

The Lord spoke to me and told me I was strong, stronger than before. I am such an empty vessel right now. This feels strange. I can see now how people go to minister to people who seem evil because they see the demons and want to cast them out. But what about all the believing Christians?

Heal me, Lord. Put bandages on my wounds. I have been in battle and I have mighty wounds that need your touch, Holy Spirit. I slept so soundly in the night.

(Note: For the 10 years that followed my deliverance, I was not able to read a secular book nor listen to secular music on the radio. The Lord was instructing me, teaching me, filling my house. Holy Spirit told me that the world had taught me for so long and that He was going to teach me now.

This was a defining moment in my life. A line drawn in the sand. It completely changed me and saved me 30 years of counseling. In an instant, God brought me up and out and then sent me to France to learn many things.)

I was urged by someone who was reading and editing this book for me to continue the story about telling my Lutheran pastors my deliverance story ...

I was attending a Lutheran church called Messiah Lutheran at the time of my deliverance and my pastors were amazing. They were kind and loving towards me.

I actually had a revelation about God's deep forgiveness towards me that changed my life forever. Holy Spirit taught me a lot while I was attending this church. He was teaching me about hearing His voice and recognizing my supernatural gifts.

One Sunday morning, I believe it was during Lent, we were going up to take communion. I saw my pastor kneel down to take the elements and I saw his prayers go upwards towards the heavens. He was saying something like ... 'Oh God, have mercy on me. How can I reach these people and show them your love?' It was such a heartfelt cry out of his heart that it grasped me in my inward parts.

The next thing that happened caught my attention. I started to see orange smoke arising from the top of his head. I didn't know what it was and just stared at it, thinking it was so beautiful. I believe it was the incense of God's fragrance as He heard my pastor's prayers.

This happened after my deliverance.

At the end of my deliverance experience, I was silent for three days. I did not speak. If anyone knows me, this is a miracle and something to take notice of. My husband noticed and confronted me. He thought I was having an affair. So, I told him the whole story. He was shocked, to say the least.

After I came out of my reverie, or whatever you want to call it, I was different, so different. Everything that had pushed me to do things and say things were gone. All gone. The tension wasn't there. There was a very deep peace inside of me, but a weird awareness on the outside. God says He will give us peace beyond all understanding and that is what this was. A peace I had never known before, but on the outside, I felt fragile and weak.

I felt the strong urge to tell my pastors about what had just happened. I booked an appointment and met with them. I was very nervous about telling them. I didn't know how they would react, but this was real, really real.

I met with them and asked if we could talk in the sanctuary under the cross hanging in the middle of the stage. I felt like I needed some coverage for some reason. My charismatic friends understood my experience, but I didn't know how my Lutheran pastors would feel about what I was going to reveal to them.

So, I told them the whole story, everything. It had only been three or four days and it was so fresh in my mind. It still is to this day.

When I finished my story, with all the details as they were fresh in my mind, I waited for a response. My two pastors are a husband-and-wife team and he went first.

He said, 'Well, that is in scripture. I believe it.'

She said, 'Wow, that is an amazing story. I want to know more.'

So, I told them all about Frank and Shirley and all my dealings with them and that they were solid people.

It was a good meeting. They were so loving and caring towards me. I could feel their genuine feelings towards me.

I didn't think anything about it until about 2 years later, I ran into my pastor in the grocery store. She told me an amazing story of how a woman had come into the church demon possessed and they didn't know what to do or how to help her. So, they arranged a meeting with Frank and Shirley and the lady was set free.

As she was sharing this story, I stood there shocked and amazed, in awe of God and His ways. Pastor told me that if I hadn't shared that story with them, they wouldn't have known what to do.

God is always good, and He will never lead you in the wrong direction. His leadership is perfect.

The fight for my Voice

Most of my life, the Lord has been leading me towards music, towards singing. I had my 1st solo in church when I was about 10 years old. In elementary school, I scored in the 99%+ category in a State musical aptitude test. I was then taken into the cafeteria. I was in the 6th grade. I was told to choose an instrument to play. I chose the bassoon, but that didn't work out.

I played the flute in middle school and was in the marching band. I was in choir and jazz choir in high school and competed on a state level. I attended Pacific Lutheran University and graduated with a Bachelor of Arts in Music, vocal performance.

This story is about the enemy trying to steal my voice. It has been the scenario my whole journey with the Lord. The movie Ariel comes to mind when Ursula wants to steal her voice. It is my voice he is after, to try to silence it.

Ten years before this incident happened, I was visiting my Mom in Danville, Virginia. The Music Director at my Mom's Baptist church had asked me to sing a solo one Sunday morning. I agreed, but had fallen sick with a bad cold upon arriving at her house. We were living in Europe at the time and the plane ride was full of sick people. Instead of bowing out saying I was sick ... because there is no way you can sing with a cold ... for some reason, I said I would go ahead and try to sing. That Sunday morning, I sang, and it was bad. It was terrible. The sounds coming out of my mouth resembled a croaking frog. I am exaggerating, but you get the picture. Even the older people in the church were coming up to me and saying in their sweet southern accent, 'Oh honey' ... it was that bad.

The enemy whispered in my ear. He whispered the same thing over the next 10 years: When you sing, you will get sick. I took that lie deep into my inner being and fear crippled me. I didn't sing for the next 10 years.

Fast forward to 10 years later to the year 2000. I was attending Messiah Lutheran church. I graduated from PLU (Pacific Lutheran University). I loved the Lutheran church services. I loved how they sang most of their services. It was beautiful and refreshing. It always brought me closer to God.

The moment of this important, powerful encounter happened right before Christmas. Messiah Lutheran church was getting ready to put on their annual Christmas pageant. A friend in the church, who has an amazing operatic voice, was organizing the pageant. My two older daughters were in the performance.

This friend approached me one Wednesday at church and asked me if I wanted to take the big solo in the middle of the performance. I immediately said no! Tangible fear gripped me the minute she asked me.

She said, 'Well, just think about it.'

My friend kept after me, gently prodding me, encouraging me and eventually I said yes. I was so scared.

I went to the practices and it felt good, but fear had me in its grip, and it was paralyzing me.

We get to the day of the performance and I am sick from the waist down and fasting on crackers and Coke, and to top it all off, my youngest daughter had a 102°F temperature. She was two years old at the time

I felt so strongly that I needed to sing that night, that I got a willing babysitter (my husband was out of town on a business trip) to watch my daughter and we went to church for the performance.

Feeling so bad and not venturing far from the bathroom, I entered the bathroom at Messiah Lutheran church. I was stressing so much, wringing my hands and sweating with the fear that this was going to be a horrible experience. As I was wrestling with the Lord, I made a deal with him.

I said, 'Tonight, I want to make a deal with you. Here's the deal: IF I bomb tonight, I will never, ever, sing again. I promise you. I won't. I will stop singing. BUT ... IF you want me to sing again, You need to make my voice glorious tonight.'

The Christmas pageant started, and it was going well. My two daughters did an amazing job.

The time came for my solo. I stood up to sing and this beautiful presence surrounded me, warm and loving. I started to sing, and I could feel this presence come in to inhabit my voice, come inside my voice. It was as if I was listening from the outside of myself and remarking at how beautiful my voice was, as if it was not my normal voice. Normally, my voice was considered kind of weak, a lack of confidence, I guess.

Standing there singing, hearing this beautiful voice come out of me that wasn't normally mine, I marveled. I was in awe.

The strength of my voice was powerful, booming. Where I had had a small and tiny voice, now there was power. Where my voice had been thin, it was rich with warmth.

I stood there amazed as I sang. It was the first time the Lord had sung through me and I was overwhelmed at His love for me. I sang and sang. It felt like the windows were going to, literally, break.

Everyone afterwards came up and said how beautiful it was. I was even asked to sing at a funeral for a long-time respected member at the church. She was so moved by my singing.

I know one thing for sure, that that was not me singing, but Holy Spirit singing through me and I was hooked. I knew God had answered my 'deal' with a resounding YES!

From my journal 5/9/01

(this was another time I had a solo while I was attending Messiah Lutheran church):

I have to tell you what happened at church last Sunday. I sang 'Yet I will Praise you". I had an urgency to sing it. I even went to Café Devine on Thursday after the whole deliverance thing and bought the music. I went to the church to practice it.

I prayed that if I was supposed to sing at 9:15 that I would be up and in good voice. Well, I was. I arrived and did a warmup. My friend came with his stand-up bass and played with me.

I had prayed the night before that Holy Spirit would come upon me and fill me and that I would no longer be there.

Well, I was singing for the first time at the 9:15 service and in the middle, I messed up. I had forgotten the words. I looked over at my friend, puzzled. I realized God had answered my prayers and I was not there, like I had disappeared. Holy Spirit had come upon me and I kept messing up the words. I guess when I ask that I should make sure Holy Spirit practices the song. It was very strange.

It is that God is showing favor on me right now and empowering me with words for so many people at church.

Today, I think I am going to tell my pastors about my deliverance story.

An Angel in New York

In 2001, I was an alto in the *Bravo! Vancouver* choir. We were going on tour to Washington D.C. and New York City in July. Everyone was excited because we were going to sing in the Lincoln Center.

Arriving in Washington D.C., we had our first concert in a church in Harlem. The band from the Duke Ellington School of the Arts was joining us on our last big piece of the program, the Duke Ellington Mass, the only mass he composed.

The young, black students strutted into the church while we were rehearsing like they owned the world. They knew they were good. Walking in cocky, heads tilted and eyes rolling, they laid eyes on our group, composed of mainly white, older singers, mostly female.

The forlorn look of 'oh man, this is going to be painful' on their faces was transparent as they swaggered into the church. Taking their places in the pews, waiting for their turn to set up and play, all slumped over, pants hanging down too low to be comfortable, they sat and listened to us rehearse. After they heard us sing, their faces changed. They could see, it might just be ok. We were good.

The concert on that first night was electric. The presence of God was so powerful. Emotions were running high. You could feel the weight of where we were and what we were singing.

Afterwards, waiting on the bus to go back to our hotel, a beautiful Black African woman jumped onto our bus in full African regal attire. Deeply affected by our concert and the presence of God, she was moved to quote Revelation 19 in boldness to us.

She boldly proclaimed, "Write this down: Blessed are those who are invited to the marriage supper of the Lamb. You are all invited to the wedding of the Lamb!! HE has made room for you. You will be at the wedding".

We were all so tired from traveling that day and then the concert that night, we all sat there speechless. After a couple of minutes, the chatter started, 'What was that? Who was that? What did she say? What does that mean? A couple of people started to criticize her.

I roared out loud, "Don't judge the messenger!"

Washington D.C. was fun and easy. Heavy laden with the choir and all our baggage on board, the bus proceeded on to New York City. Excitement permeated the group.

Our minds were on singing at the Lincoln Center. Upon arriving in the city, confusion and hostility met us; the comparison was striking. New York felt hostile, aggressive, and hard.

Settling into our hotel rooms, my two new friends and I set out to roam the city before the concert that evening. The entrance to the subway was tricky to find. We descended the stairs to see if we could catch a train. Confusion struck us immediately. With one line going one way at a certain specific time and the other train going the other direction at different times, we couldn't figure out which train to take.

An officer on the platform tried to explain the rules, but it was so complicated that none of us understood a thing he was saying. He told us to take the next train coming up. It would take us the right way.

The train came into the station and stopped. Immediately, my two friends jumped on it. I jumped on a little late because I didn't believe that the officer was right about the direction we were to take. That split second of indecision and my left hand got caught in the door as it was shutting over my knuckles.

As I was trying to pull my hand through the rubber door locks, my wedding ring got stuck and broke in half as my hand slid painfully through the locked subway doors of the train. It all happened so fast. My hand was scratched up and bloody and starting to swell. My wedding ring was cracked but still intact on my finger.

Not believing what had just happened, we rode a few more stops and got off. I found a place to clean up my hands and we took the stairs and headed outside. We were lost.

Standing there, a sinking feeling fell on us. There were hordes of people everywhere going every which way, and the three of us stood there trying to figure out what to do. Tired and hurt, all I wanted to do was go back to the hotel.

As we stood there facing each other discussing the situation, desperation creeping into our speech, a very old, very small man, dressed in a rust and black tweed, three-piece suit, complete with handkerchief, hat and umbrella hanging off his left arm, approached us from the side. He seemed to come out of nowhere and was completely out of place. It was like having someone step out of a 1940s English movie and come and speak to us.

Time seemed to stand still and I wondered if we had entered into a dream. It was all so unusual, surreal. Deep down, I knew that everything was going to be alright, and that help had arrived.

He said softly in a very heavy, high British accent, 'Excuse me. May I be of some assistance?'

Mystified by his appearance, the three of us looked at each other. There was a long moment of silence before we said in desperation, "Yes, we're lost."

Without a thought or a waiver, never asking us where we were wanting to go or who we were, he said intensely, in a strong and powerful voice, "You need the #52 bus. It will take you where you want to go. Now hurry along. It is right over there.", as he pointed to a bus pulling in at a stop nearby. For some reason, we trusted this old man, his kindness. We knew he was safe and had come with the answer.

Acting quickly on his words, we ran towards the #52 bus.

Wanting to thank him, all three of us turned around at the same time and realized our friend was nowhere to be found. He just wasn't there. Knowing we had but seconds to catch the bus, wonder filled our thoughts and we started to question what had just happened as we ran towards the bus. Excitement filled our speech, "That was amazing! Mind-blowing! Was he an angel? Where was he? Where did he go?"

Marveling, we realized that God had sent an angel to help us find our way back to the hotel. We rejoiced, "Unbelievable! How can that be? It had to be an angel! THAT WAS GOD!" It filled our conversations for the rest of the trip.

It's Your move, Lord

In the Fall of 2000, my husband came to me and asked if I was up for him looking for a way into moving back to Europe to work.

I said, 'No, absolutely not.'

I told him, 'Now was not the time to ask me, but to try me at another time.'

He came back two weeks later, and I didn't object, but gave him a feeble maybe.

He was off and running.

I honestly thought this would never happen.

There was a job in Geneva, Switzerland, that opened up, but we didn't get it.

I stipulated that I would only think about going if we were Expats, meaning that we would have a house, not an apartment, and that we would live amongst Anglophones, English-speaking people. I put other stipulations. I had a long list. I thought this was never going to go through. They would never send a Frenchman into his own country as an Expat. Never. I was comfortable with where I was.

That winter, something came up in France. The job would be a big promotion for Francois, and he asked for an FSC Expat contract (Foreign Service Contract). This is not normally done and doesn't really make any sense, sending a Frenchman as an expat into his own country. Normally, this is done to alleviate any cultural adjustments that will happen in the 'new' country.

Much to my shock and amazement, Hewlett-Packard said yes!

O, how I grappled with this. I realized that everyone was going to benefit from this move but me: Francois in his big, new job; the children becoming completely bilingual and reconnecting with their French side of themselves. But me? What was I going to gain by going back to this country that I viewed as hostile? I felt like a sacrificial lamb and I was not happy about it.

At my Wednesday morning group, there was much prayer put into this for my family and me. The ladies did a 24-hour prayer watch for my situation to see what God was saying. They all received words and scripture from the Lord on this. Three of the ladies got the book of Esther. Two of them got Jeremiah 29:11-14, that God's plans for us are good. This is my forever verse.

Most all agreed, though, that it was the Lord asking me to lay down my desires and be obedient. It didn't matter if we went or not, what mattered was I was to be obedient to His wishes and desires.

Most of the women said that God had already gone before me and all I had to do was walk into it. I held on to these words throughout the whole journey.

All this spiritual stuff was new to me and asking God for things was new to me. I didn't know what to do or how to ask. I didn't want to go back to Paris, as I knew what to expect. I had lived in France already twice before and I dreaded the thought of living there again. I felt I wasn't hard enough, strong enough to go back to Paris, to big city living and the harshness of that beautiful city. I felt fragile and weak, like I would be eaten alive.

Every time I would pray, I would hear 'GO', but my mind would ask one more time, 'Lord, do you want us to go to France?'

The pastors at my Lutheran church prayed for me and laid hands on me and got the same scriptures as some of the ladies in the group; but I wanted to ask one last time over and over again, 25,000 times I asked. Maybe God will say no this time.

At this same time, Francois' Aunt and Uncle came to visit us from Boulogne, a city just on the outskirts of Paris. They both were able to answer all my questions and it was a blessing that they were 'coincidentally' there at this precise time. I knew it was no coincidence. God had sent them to bring comfort and confidence to me.

I remember so clearly sitting in church on Good Friday, as they reenacted in a powerful service, Jesus' last days before His crucifixion. I was sobbing so hard during the whole service and crying out to God. 'Please take this cup from me, Lord. I do not want to go!"

I remember Pastor Peter looked at me funny as he was preaching. I really needed some answers. I was wrestling hard with God in what He was asking me to do.

That Sunday morning, Easter morning, I came downstairs early in the morning before everyone had gotten up, to thank Jesus and pray just this one last time, like David, for peace and contentment in this situation and an answer if we were to go or not.

I got down on my knees in the family room and prayed. I took my bible to do the 'open-the-bible-and-point–your-finger-to-scripture' routine that we are told not to do.

I said, 'Lord, this is the last time I will ask this of you and please give me a direct answer.'

I will accept your answer.

With my eyes closed and on my knees, I opened my Bible and laid it down on the carpet. I lifted my hand high above my head, index finger pointed up, ready to stab the page. I said a small little prayer then slowly drove my pointed index finger down and it landed on the page. I waited for a moment with my eyes closed, holding my breath. I didn't want to open my eyes.

When I opened them, my finger was resting exactly on the word 'GO' (in Jer. 13).

Then I read the passage of one of the ladies of my group, Jeremiah 29, and I knew for sure the Lord was taking us to France. I had complete conviction and confirmation. My spirit knew it, but my head was having a lot of trouble getting around this fact. This trip was all about obedience. Was I willing to totally surrender and go wherever God wanted me to go? Was I willing to pay the price? The Holy Spirit was given so that we might live out our lives in over our heads.

The wheels were now set in motion to go. In June of 2001, Francois and I arranged to go on a preview trip. This is where you visit the place where you are going to move to and give them a yes or no. Everyone knows that you don't go on a pre-view trip and say no. The real goal of the trip is to pick out a house and set up schools for the kids.

The house experience was a test of faith. There were several ladies in my Wednesday group who had received the same thing from the Lord, and basically, it was that God had already gone before us, and all we had to do was walk into it. I took this literally, and I was not disappointed.

We had 5 days in Paris to get everything in order. I went around with a relocation lady named Anne, who had organized everything for us: appointments to see houses and all the schools in the area, plus showing me around where all the shopping areas were.

The move was a 'GO'.

The house in Bailly, France

This is the testimony of our family moving to France in 2001, 2 weeks before 9/11 and the Twin Towers in Manhattan falling. God moved mountains to get us to France and His timing was impeccable.

From my journal 6-22-01

The whole house-hunting experience was a test of faith. We had already seen about four houses, and even though every one of them would have been acceptable, none of them were just exactly right ... until we arrived in Bailly.

All morning in the car, I had started to become discouraged. We had been house hunting for a couple of days, and I was thinking maybe the Lord hadn't gone before us to prepare the way, that maybe He had forgotten about me and that all the prayers weren't right. They were good intentions, but not true. Doubt started to creep in.

We arrived in Bailly. I knew this town. Our English-speaking dentist had been located here when we lived in France the last time we lived here. There was also an English-speaking playgroup that met here and our vet had his office here.

So, I'm in the car with our relocation person, Anne. She was amazing, taking me everywhere, explaining everything, really helping me out.

When we first turned down the small, narrow, curvy road lined with walls covered in ivy, my heart started to beat a little faster. Memories started to flood my mind about this town. I could tell the Lord was trying to get my attention. I sat up and started to pay attention.

I had told Anne about all the prayers and prophetic words about us moving to France. I also told her about the house and that I would 'know'. I was starting to trust in His faithfulness and realize He was for me and wouldn't let me down.

The prayers that supported me on this trip were that the Lord had gone before me and made a place for us and all I had to do was walk into it. I was waiting for this.

We parked the car on the other side of the street and got out.

A dog was barking, and I thought, 'Oh no, I will never be able to live near that!'

We'd had a neighbor with an annoying dog that barked all day long while she was at work!

Well, it turned out that the barking dog belonged to the people who owned the house we were looking at, so the dog would not be there! Problem solved.

I looked at the house from the outside and it looked nice enough. We rang the doorbell and waited for the people to come out. We entered the gate that surrounded the property and started to walk up to the front door.

Discouragement was creeping into my thoughts again and I was thinking, maybe He hasn't gone before me to prepare the way. Doubt was creeping in fast and then we arrived on the doorstep.

The moment I walked across the threshold of the house, my whole body filled with goosebumps and I KNEW this was our house!

I had been telling Anne, the relocation person, all about the prophetic words about God making a way for us.

I said to Anne, 'I think this is THE house!'

She said, 'Don't you want to at least look around?'

I said, 'No, this is it!'

She said, 'Ok! But let's look around.'

I said, 'Ok.'

Walking through the house, I could feel it was ours. The beautiful white tiles all over the downstairs floors, to the green and yellow and white tiles in the kitchen, to the enormous fireplace in the middle of the living room, to the 4 spacious bedrooms upstairs, it was perfect. It was everything I had asked for on my list of things that I wanted. It was even perfect for the buses my two older daughters would take to get to their respective schools, the bus stop for the two of them only being a five-minute walk from the house.

I started crying and I told Anne this was the house that I had been waiting for. I knew it was the one.

This house turned out to be an amazing house, twenty minutes from Paris, well placed, right in-between the two schools.

Two years before we arrived, the owner, who used to be the Head Coach for the Paris-St Germain soccer team, had spent a lot of money completely remodeling the house. This house was brand new, new kitchen, new carpet, and new tiles everywhere. It was gorgeous! It was a King's house close to Paris.

This house was used by the Lord and many supernatural encounters happened here. I had a morning meeting at my house every Monday morning. It was such a perfect place. The abundance of having a 2500 square foot house that is close to Paris is unheard of.

But God!

A side note: While we were there at the house, I got a call from the school where my middle daughter was supposed to attend. We had visited them the day before and they had said there wasn't any room for her. They called to say that circumstances had come up and they had room for her at the school. This is the best middle school in France: Lycee International in St Germain-en-Laye.

*Journal entry August 1, 2001,
before we moved:*

I am sitting here in the residence Inn crying my eyes out over the end of everything, leaving everything, my friends, my life here in the US. Things are happening just as God said they would. The move went so smoothly, and everything fell right into place, just like He said. We have all been so calm and reassured by God's presence and authority on all of this. God's timing is so perfect. He is awesome.

I am so glad I went on the Bravo Choir tour. (This tour occurred 10 days before we were to move. We sang in Washington DC and New York City in the Lincoln Center.) *I met some friends, and we spent a lot of time together. We had so much fun just being alive and getting no sleep. Every night we were up and going out and not really doing anything but talking and laughing and horsing around.*

The concerts were such spiritual experiences for me, especially the first one at the Nativity Catholic church. Bonding with the audience like we did. Then the woman prophesied on the bus, Revelations and the Lincoln Center concert.

I understood a great deal about myself upon returning. I seemed to have rediscovered a part of me that was hidden, and I really like that person. I realize that situations and people and family and husbands and children can manipulate and mold a woman without her realizing this is happening. I never realized how much I let that happen. I had somehow, in the midst of all of it, of taking care of others, I had lost myself... and on this amazing journey, I found a part of myself again.

Journal entry 8/28/01:

Our suffering changes us. Only through our suffering can we know what is good. Our suffering changes what we are and who we are. It changes our destiny of who we will become. Through God's discipline and pruning, we are changed. We become who God wants us to be.

Journal testimony from the move 9/18/01:

Well, we are here in Bailly, France. The house is pretty much in order, not much else to finish now. The house turned out to be perfectly located: close to Francois' job, right in between the girls' two schools and a lot of English speakers in the area.

The shipment came and was in perfect order. It came on the only day that Francois could be home and the week before school started. What a blessing!

We were able to sell our station wagon to a pastor in Portland.

There was a lady who had stopped by to see us off and she was short of money that month. I was able to give her six bags of groceries the day before we left.

I had been here in the new house for about a week and I was in the middle of unpacking. I was tired and fed up and lonely and not liking it in France, despite everything being perfect. Just when I was at my depths of sadness and couldn't take it anymore, my friend called from the States. I was so surprised and happy. It was just what I needed. God knows just what we need at the right time.

She had tried to call all weekend and had the number wrong. Finally, she got the right number and called just when I needed it. We talked for over two hours.

I was saying how I wanted to go home and have my old life back, and sing in Bravo, and to go to my church, and to my ladies' group, and see my old friends. She said that it was worth it – if it was just for one person.

She then told me the story about how she had felt the same exact way when she moved to the States a couple of years ago from Europe. The same as I felt that day when she called me, not thinking it was worth it. The Lord led her to this ladies' group. The night before she went, she had just finished telling her sister how it wasn't worth it moving to the States. That was the same day I came to the group for the first time, and I told everyone how enlightened and awake and on fire I had become.

You see, this was my friend who had lied to me so that God could position me for my destiny moving forward. My friend went home and called her sister and told her it was worth it for just one.

I then realized that I was her one soul and that I was worth it. I cried for hours.

Another revelation I have just had. I couldn't figure out God's timing on the 2001 tragedy in New York and DC (twin towers/Pentagon).

Why was it only after we had been here in France for two weeks did this whole thing happened? I could have been of better assistance in the States.

And then I realized that it happened perfectly. It is a sign that I am in the right place. If this had happened earlier, while we were still in the States, it would have prevented us from moving. It would have been a definite sign for us not to move. But the fact that it happened two weeks after we were safely in place is a sign from God that we are where we should be.

From my journal

This is right after our move to France and the 9/11 terrorist attack:

2:14am (9-20-01)

I was awakened by 'ARISE' - SHOUTING IN MY HEAD ... hard to get up ...door bangs.

I get up. Lots of weird, heavy air. I pray and go upstairs ...the window opens suddenly.

I say out loud, "I'm not scared' and it stops.

9-20-01

(This was when we were in France. We had just moved there two weeks after 9/11 and I was just learning about prophecy.)

I think I had another revelation. Before I left the US, I kept telling everyone that something was going to happen, and I wasn't going to be there to see it. I thought it was something to do with the Church.

I told the Music Minister at Messiah Lutheran, my church at the time before we moved, how I saw people lining up by the 100s entering the back of the church entrance. It seemed the line went all the way down the street, and they were coming and coming. I thought this had to do with the 'something that I was going to miss'.

But could the Twin Towers tragedy be the big thing that was going to happen, and I wasn't going to be there to watch?

(I watched the Twin Towers fall from the TV in my living room in Paris, France. I was not in the US to witness this.)

Could my thoughts and words for the church have been about the hijacking? I got a call from a friend and she was telling me all about the feelings in the States after Tuesday's events and how her church was packed on Sunday.

Could this be the 100s coming to Messiah Lutheran?

Could God have bestowed upon me such a thing?

Glory to God.

Saturday 9-29-01

I feel a certain peace descending on me.

Joyce Meyer's book, 'Battlefield of the mind', is really helping me.

I feel that I need to be patient, not only that, but have a good attitude about it all. To wait on God, be happy in every moment because every moment that passes is gone forever and we can never get it back.

God, teach me to wait on You in reverence and contentment.

All that really matters in this life is You God and Your will.

I humble myself before You God and wait on You to lift me up.

I am weak but there is such power and strength in our weakness, as we wait on You God, You fill all those empty places as we wait and abide in You.

Help me to abide in You.

Oh Lord, stay close to me. Whisper in my ears all your Love for me.

Comfort me in my time of need, Lord

Stay close and wrap me in Your protective cloud of Love.

Make me to feel Your presence.

Show me my future God.

Give me the Spirit of Knowledge and Wisdom that I might use this all for your Glory.

Oh God, don't leave now, I depend on You and not on my own fleshly body.

Stay with me.

Guide me.

Lead me straight through the narrow gate.

Keep evil from me, far from me, far from my thoughts and doings.

Oh Lord, You are Faithful, Faithful!

10-9-01 – Wednesday morning

I heard the voice of God!

He said Prophecy – 'The time for silence is over, stand firm and steadfast with your armor tight and go forth and proclaim Truth. Be bold, now the time to be silent is finished!'

A very loud voice in my head. I asked ... Who is this?

He said 'THE LORD YOUR GOD'

Anointed for worship
at CVC in France

In August of 2001, two weeks before 9/11, we moved to France.

I settled into a bilingual charismatic church, led by a Pastor from Louisiana, after being in a Baptist church for a couple of months.

God had been moving powerfully in supernatural experiences and encounters the entire year before we moved, and Holy Spirit wasn't letting up.

Most of my spiritual journey had been in a Lutheran church and singing hymns and no spiritual movement at all, or at least that I was aware of.

The first Sunday that I attended my new church, I sensed an immense urge to go up and grab the microphone and sing. I could feel the pull in my spirit. So much so that I had to hold onto my chair to prevent myself from going up there and doing just that.

After the service, I felt compelled to go and speak with the worship leader.

This is what came out of my mouth in French:

I said, 'You guys need a female singer, and I am it!'

I was shocked at my boldness, but I could feel Holy Spirit all over it and in control, because I never would have done that!

The worship leader responded, 'Ok, come Saturday for practice. You can sing on Sunday'.

I went to my car, dumbstruck and sat there for a while and pondered what God was up to. I was stunned at the boldness and courage Holy Spirit had supplied me with. I was excited and scared all at the same time.

Sunday came and the agenda was to sing six songs. I only knew one of them and they were all in French!

Now mind you, I had never 'worshiped' before.

I had only sung solos in church. I didn't know what that meant or how to do it. I also, didn't know what to expect.

God had been moving so powerfully in my life, bringing me totally out of my comfort zone, but in a great state of peace.

I was open to anything and trusting Him.

Sunday morning, the worship starts and before I know it, the power of God hits me hard, and I can barely stand up.

His presence is so thick and strong and has overcome me and my physical body.

I am holding onto the microphone stand and barely able to stand up or keep it together.

I 'disappear' into this place in the spirit, into another realm in space and time, taken up in the spirit.

I have never been to this place nor seen it before.

It is a heavenly place I can tell, a heavenly realm.

It feels holy and I can see melodies everywhere.

I am floating and feeling like my body has been taken over, because I am no longer in my body.

I am not sure where I am, but I don't care. It is amazing.

I don't know what I am singing.

I am not aware of myself on the earth or my feet on the ground.

I am not there and I can hear the beauty in the spontaneous, antiphonal singing that is coming out of my mouth.

Someone has taken over my voice and is singing through me.

I don't recognize my own voice.

I can feel this huge, gigantic angel standing behind me, hovering protectively over my back , pouring buckets of oil, anointing my head.

I can feel the oil drip down my hair and all over my head and drip down, covering my entire body.

I hear the voice of the Lord say:

'I am anointing you today for worship. I am anointing you as a worship leader. Everything up until this moment has been preparation for right now, this moment.'

In a flash of an instant, I see a timeline appear in the spirit that stretches from the time I was born up through my entire life. It is showing me how He has led me through every single year of my entire life up until that very moment in time.

Immediately, I understand everything in my life and how it has all worked out for my good.

All the dots fall into place and I can see my life's journey and I understand everything. The journey through my life's timeline was instant. I knew everything in one moment.

Remember, this is all happening while I am singing!

Worship is finishing and I 'come to'.

I come back to earth, to the ground I am standing on.

I am hanging on the microphone stand, my head bowed to the side of it.

I don't know what has just happened or what I have just sung.

I am not sure what has been going on, but I know it was a powerful moment for me.

I looked straight at the worship leader and said, 'Wow, that was powerful!'

He says, 'Yeah, that was good.'

I understood right then that this was just for me and it was personal.

I have trouble walking from the weight of His presence on me and I crawl back on all fours to my seat and sit down, as the whole church watches me.

I had had some deep pain in my middle back for a couple of weeks and my back gets healed that morning. ... and out of all that starts the ministry that God gave me in France called Unity in Christ.

The weeks that followed, I was a different person. There was a powerful anointing that I could feel and lean into. I started having an angel show up when I would sing and he would show me, in the spirit, the melody that he would want me to sing.

In this ascended place, I would see him frolicking over the mountains and into the fields and leaving melodic notes behind him for me to sing. He was so playful and joyous and really loved what he was doing.

I also started to write out my Book of Remembrance, detailing out every year of my life and what had happened. It was a powerful journey through this timeline to see how God's hand had been on my life throughout it all, even when I didn't even know it or see it or even know Him.

He had me in His grasp the whole time and still does.

Beginning of Unity in Christ

Taken from my journal:

Oh Lord, you have just shown me something grand. I feel you are speaking to my heart. The other day, a friend brought up the subject of unity and that I should get a band together with musicians from all the different churches – I think she is right.

Some churches are already getting together to meet and discuss unity. I have all the necessary ingredients to bring it about, with congregations participating from several churches.

A worship night where all come together to praise the Lord-Jesus Christ in unity, confirm our fundamental beliefs of God, Jesus, the Holy Spirit – three in one Unity!

We are all the Body of Christ, each individual member making up the Whole Body of Christ (Romans 12:4-6).

Each church has its function but should unite on the basis of Love, Joy and the Grace of God and the Lord Jesus Christ and our helper and friend, Holy Spirit.

The husband of a friend of mine who was there at my church when that big angel poured the anointing oil on my head called me the next day and suggested we meet up to get together and jam to see what would happen.

He and another guy had been talking about getting a band together to worship.

.... Well, I haven't been able to sleep because I am so excited for this worship thing. I've been waking up in the night 2-3 times. The Lord seems to be filling me with energy. I can't wait to see what God is going to do!

Last Sunday at church, something wonderful happened – God showed up in a big way!

The worship team was on fire and people were clapping and jumping up and down and dancing all over the place. The drummer went nuts! It was beautiful.

The three of us met for the first time and it was magical.

We played for 2 ½ hours without even stopping for a drink of water!

There was something about the three of us, coming together, from three different churches, that propelled us into the spirit.

We were incredible together. The synchronization was electric.

Our voices together and the way we followed each other was amazing!

I can't quite describe how that all felt. It was like sweet honey, all warm and good.

Holy Spirit was all in our unity.

The next day after we met, Bill Yount, a prophet, posted on the Elijah List this message:

'As streams of Worship flowing out of different churches were coming together, I saw whole cities plunged beneath a great cleansing flood as darkness began pursuing God's enemies!

I heard the enemy scream at these streams. 'How can it be – worship teams are breaking loose out of the boundaries of their own churches and flowing together corporately with other worship teams? We must stop their anointings from mixing together. Their strengths will be contagious to one another and their weaknesses will be drowned in the presence of their God as He inhabits their praises?'

The enemy continues shouting orders to regroup his confused demons. 'If they 'cross-pollinate', they will find 'Honey in the Rocky places' of their churches and personal lives. This is not the way it's supposed to be! We must increase our distractions to keep them separated and isolate them, consuming them with their own individual problems and personal struggles.'

The enemy spoke now saying, 'Stop the flow! – Stop the flow!' we're losing focus. As they are flowing together, it's like they are moving in the Spirit and leaving no forwarding address! If they continue to come together, we will surely lose sight of them as they become one. And if we lose these churches through corporate worship, we will surely lose this city!'

In the Spirit, I heard chains snapping, fetters breaking, and strongholds being demolished. Wicked Spirits in high (governmental) places were weakening as corporate worship was rising higher – thrusting upwards like a 'spiritual sword' severing the jugular vein of the Prince of the Power of the Air over cities and regions.'

... I couldn't believe it when I saw this prophetic word!

I saw it on Monday in my emails!

God is amazing the way he puts information in our paths like that for confirmation and encouragement!'

During this time, the Lord was using the Elijah List to teach me that what I was hearing in the spirit was correct.

I would receive revelation and then the next day, or the next week, He would confirm what He was saying to me.

I was practicing hearing His voice and trying to be obedient.

I was praying, 'Lord, let me be so close to your heart and your voice that I don't have to ask if it is you or not, so that I can be swift in my obedience.'

Obedience is the key, not sacrifice.

November 30th worship night at CVC

From my journal:

Well, we just had a worship night last night, a Thanksgiving worship.

I really don't know what to think because this one was going so well.

It was our first night at my church and a French/English night.

We felt we were stepping out going bilingual.

There were to be 5 of us on the team.

The very night before our worship night, our keyboard player's wife tried to commit suicide.

*It had to do with things that were **not** connected to us, but past history with her and the church we were playing at and the leaders' abusive behavior.*

(One of the things the Lord was showing me is that what we do in the spirit for Him is not child's play. There are dangerous consequences sometimes.)

It was a devastating moment for my friend … and for all of us.

It was so tragic.

We were in shock.

She ended up being Ok physically, but the emotional turmoil on her was great. My friend ended up dropping out of our group for good.

That Saturday morning for our practice, I arrived at the church and couldn't make it up the stairs. I was weeping so hard. It was such a mixture of things – weeping for her, hurting for him, remembering my own self years ago in the kitchen of my house in Tacoma contemplating slitting my wrists … and then his not being able to join us.

I felt the enemy had won and felt like my feet had been kicked out underneath me.

I am not sure how we all came to this conclusion, but we all decided to go ahead with the worship night.

We decided to praise Jesus in the midst of this great tragedy and sorrow.

I had said to myself that Saturday afternoon that 'I wasn't going to do another worship night'.

It was just too hard.

I was going to rest now and pray about all of this because it hurt too much. I am going to wait on you Lord and let you do the work, if you want this to continue, you have to do something. You take over. I can't do it. You orchestrate it now. I will wait on You. My heart is too heavy.'

I arrived that Saturday night and my heart was so heavy.

I really didn't want to do it.

I wasn't sure how I was going to sing.

My heart hurt so much, and I couldn't stop crying.

There were about 50/60 people that came, and that was a very good turnout. That is a big crowd in France.

But God.

He really used us all.

He really used me and worked something deep in my heart.

I was so broken.

I was in great voice that night. I could feel the power in my voice. I felt His presence so strong and really working through me, singing through me.

It was powerful.

He says He will be the strength in our weakness.

We had great songs picked out. I wanted it to be different than it was. I wanted my friend there. I wanted it to be about us singing and not just me. I had prayed that the Lord would make it the way He wanted it.

There were some ladies dancing in the back.

One lady was crying her eyes out.

I had my eyes closed for a long while and when I opened them, I saw many people on their knees, hands in the air.

People were getting touched.

The air was electric with His presence.

The Lord was moving powerfully that night.

I had had a vision in prayer a few weeks prior to this.

I saw a cellar door in the ground open up and a dove flew out.

Also, I had the feeling that there were closed doors that we needed to push open. I felt like groaning but didn't because no one else was and I thought it wasn't allowed.

The Thursday before that Saturday, while in prayer at my bible school, I saw many doors lining a hallway ... old doors ...ancient doors.

There were many of them. I knew they were old and had been there a long time and at one time they had been open, but were now closed and we needed to open them.

The next day at bible school, during our prayer of consecration, the Lord showed me MY ancient door from before the foundations of the world and that this held all provision for me and that He was going to open it.

As He was showing me and as He was opening up the revelation, I could barely stand up. I was hanging onto the windowsill and weeping. I could not handle the amount of love He was showing me. He gave me a glimpse!

The next day, the Lord said to me:_

You are not to be discouraged!

You are not to hurry.

You are to sit, like a chicken on a lot of eggs and warm them.

(I saw a basket with a lot of eggs, and I knew that these were the plans and people God was getting ready)

This is preparation for you.

Don't let the devil try to hurry you and get you ahead of me.

Everything is in order.

Hearts are being prepared

People are ready.

I am opening up the ancient door of your inheritance and provision is waiting before the foundation of the world.

The door is opening, and it is flooding out.

I will prepare the way for everything.

Many times, there would be supernatural occurrences in our practices and our worship gatherings:

When we would practice, Holy Spirit's presence would be so strong. It would take me away into another dimension and the hours would disappear. Time would cease to exist.

One time when we were in the Salle Polyvalente in Boulogne, after a particularly difficult evening that was hard and blissful at the same time, we discovered gold dust on our equipment. We even went to the janitor to see if he knew what it was.

Many times, I would hear a bass player when we didn't have one.

I would hear Choirs of Angels singing with us sometimes.

Sometimes I would ask the Lord not to bring anyone, as our practices were incredible.

One time at a worship gathering in Marly-le-Roi, that was a very difficult evening to begin with.

While we were practicing, I felt Jesus come through the door of the church and walk down the aisle.

You could feel His weighty presence.

As He got close to us, He turned to the right and the hem of His garment swished by me and a wind knocked me back into my chair.

We all looked at each other like ... what was that???

*Footnote-Domata Bible school was a nine-month intensive Bible school, based out of Kenneth Hagins ministry for people on the mission field. It's a two-year course condensed down to nine months.

Key in the Quiche

Some of you may know that I have lived in France three times. Three times a charm, they say.

The last time that we lived there, the Lord gave me a ministry. We didn't know it was a ministry. We ended up calling it Unity in Christ. We had all kinds of amazing things go on.

One day, my two friends and I were picking up an Evangelist from the airport. We were going to have her come back to my British friend's house for some tea and quiche. The Evangelist was going to stay with someone else. I can't remember who.

This Evangelist was one of the loyal people who used to come to France to minister. Not many people came to France to minister. It's a rough place. They would come, get smacked down by the enemy and never come back.

France is called the graveyard of ministry.

My word of warning is to never go anywhere unless the Lord directs you to go. He will make a way where there is no way and keep you safe when He sends you.

Africans come. They come and they do business. They have experience with darkness and know how to deal with 'stuff'.

We're at the airport picking up the Evangelist. She gets in the car and she starts going on and on and on about three things.

I said, 'Ok what are the three things?'

She says, 'Well, we're just going to concentrate on one thing.'

I said, 'That's not fair'.

She says, 'We're going to concentrate on one thing.'

She starts talking about Communion. She's going on and on and on about communion.

This was in 2002, BEFORE we were all talking about how important it is to take Communion.

She's going on and on and on about how it is the most important thing to do. How it is the number #1 thing to do. She wouldn't tell us anything more and said she would share the next day on its importance.

We're in the car and we are all getting excited.

She says, 'Well, I can't tell you everything.'

We arrive at my friend's house. The Evangelist brings all her stuff in. We are all getting settled and setting the table and getting ready to have lunch and break bread together. There is an excitement in the air.

My friend takes the quiche out of the oven and sets it on the table. There was salad as well.

We each got a piece of the quiche and some salad. French people drink wine with their meals. We always had wine with our meal before our prayer meetings at my French church.

We each have a piece of our quiche and we are eating it and my friend asks if anyone wants another piece.

I said, 'Well, I do.'

Everyone wants another piece.

My friend grabs the knife and goes to cut the quiche, but she can't.

She says, 'What is going on?'

She keeps trying to push the knife down into the quiche, but she can't cut the quiche.

There is something blocking her from cutting through the quiche to get a slice.

She says, 'Something is in the quiche!'

She digs her fingers in the quiche and feels an object.

It is a key.

It is about 3 inches long.

It is an ancient-looking key and has the number #1 engraved on it.

She pulls the key out of the quiche.

I jump up and yell ... 'Oh my God! It's the key! It's a sign!'

And then the room went crazy!

Everyone jumped up and started yelling!

I am not sure what happened after that, but we were lost in the Spirit for four hours.

The first hour was laughing, laughing, laughing, jumping, jumping, jumping.

We got tired and laid on the floor and laughed and laughed and laughed.

We then got up and ran around outside in the yard, holding our pants and skirts up as we ran, and we ran and ran and ran and ran.

We come back in the house and we sit on the floor and we are all laughing and talking.

Four hours went by.

Four hours!

Totally drunk in the spirit.

Four hours!

Four hours in His presence.

In His Glory.

Outside of us, not coming from the inside, but from the outside.

In His Glory.

We all started to come out of it saying ... 'Whoa!! What?!

It's like 6 or 7:00 at night. I have to get home.'

We all looked at each other and said ... 'What was that? '

Intrigued, we went into the kitchen to try to see where the key had come from. My friend had made the quiche and swore she had not put a key in there! We were all sure someone had put the key in there. Someone must have put it there!

We looked all over the kitchen, in the cupboards, over the stove, behind the door, we looked everywhere, trying to figure out how a key could've fallen into the quiche.

We were all perplexed!

Then we all drove to my friend's house, who had made the quiche, to see if we could find a place in the kitchen where the key could've fallen from.

'Oh, it must've fallen from somewhere into the batter and into the quiche', but we couldn't find it.

We looked to see if there was a ledge or something it could've rested on ... but no ledge.

We were in awe of what Holy Spirit did that day.

Activation

Now, everyone is talking about keys and there is something significant about that, always has been.

The Lord has talked to me about keys for a long time.

Ancient keys.

Ancient doors.

Ancient wells.

It feels like it is time.

It feels like it is time to open them up.

Put your Key in the lock in the door.

Open it and push the door open.

Let's do that.

Let's activate.

Everyone close your eyes.

Just imagine in your hand ... just ask the Lord... Holy Spirit give me a key.

Give me a key to open up my destiny.

Hold your hand out and receive your key.

If you already have one that is great.

Receive your key.

If you want to, ask Him what it is to be used for... and then go open that door!

Take your key and insert it in the lock of your ancient door of provision.

Thank you, Jesus.

From my activation journal:

Wednesday 1/15/2014:

I was listening to a Podcast and the speaker starts talking about the angelic canopy in heaven and an angel called Metatron, chief angel.

.... I immediately got taken back in the spirit to France and the key in the quiche incident.

It is interesting that there were 4 of us there – creating a door – a Dalit. The key had the #1 on it and it was ancient, and we all went into an encounter together for four hours!

Was it the angel Metatron who put the key in there?

It is still a mystery to me.

Deliverance

November 20th, 2001, in France

From my journal:

Thank you, Lord, – I give you all the praise and glory.

My friends came to pray for me and I ended up getting delivered. I had been feeling a heavy presence of rejection and something else from earlier in my life – possibly from the time at PLU. From my past experiences, I knew that I needed help from my friends.

As my friends prayed over me, there was deliverance from the spirit of rejection, witchcraft (medians), spirit of fear – fear of man, anger ... Thank you Jesus.

(Some information concerning the medians and witchcraft - My mom, even though she was a Christian, a true Baptist, used to visit psychics and tarot readers every once in a while. I believe she was wanting the supernatural prophetic knowing that was yearning deep down in her that was a part of her inheritance. She was visiting me in France and we went to the big hypermarket grocery store. There was a psychic who had a tent in the little strip mall there

and my mom paid for me to have a reading. The psychic spoke about the future birth of my 3rd child. Told me not to have another baby, that it would be dangerous. I have to say that she was correct in her reading, because there was a dangerous moment in the birth of my 3rd child that was a life or death situation. I was glad that I was aware and that everything turned out ok for everyone. Everything was working for my good and the good of my baby!)

I had a vision while my friends were praying:

I could see, in the spirit, clouds like shifting sand and the sand was blowing across these clouds ... and I saw Jesus with His hands stretched out towards me saying, 'Come to me'.

He was so loving and warm, and I knew everything would be alright in His arms.

After all the prayer, I felt such peace.

I saw a white dove flapping its lovely, grand, golden wings and flying away from me. I knew we were finished.

While they were praying, my friend had a vision of my Father right after I was born.

He was bending over my crib and crying tears of joy over me ... something so new and beautiful.

He was delighted that I was born.

I had such joy afterwards. I felt so light and free.

I saw a room filled with huge candelabras, gold ones, with huge candles and they were all lit.

The room was aglow with these candles and I felt such joy.

January 26th, 2002

From my journal:

A prayer...

We were made to feel like this.

We were all made to receive this blessing and be filled.

We were all made to praise Yahweh, to worship Him with everything that we have, with open hearts, with open minds, we are to be open channels.

We are to pour forth everything.

Yahweh is waiting to fill us every day.

He has more than we can possibly stand.

We were made to be like this.

We were made to act this way.

We were made to worship Yahweh.

We were made to receive Holy Spirit.

My soul sings.

My spirit rises.

We were made to feel this power in us and then use it.

Oh Abba, how You fill us.

An answer to prayer for marriage

Journal February 2002

So, another sleepless night praising Abba!

Tuesday a prophetess came to my friend's house. She wasn't a very good preacher. I wasn't too keen on her voice. I was a little checked out.

When she asked for us to close our eyes and if we had a word from God, I had one, but I couldn't say it out loud, couldn't voice it.

She went on to talk about Africa and the healings going on there.

Then I gave the word I got from the Lord: **'Watch, wait and see what my mighty hand will do '.**

I think Yahweh wanted to show me my gift.

I had invited a friend to the meeting.

While we were singing and worshiping, I couldn't sing. It was like a hand was over my mouth. I was so tired and I just kept my mouth closed and listened. I felt everyone wanting me to sing, to lead, but I felt if I did, it wouldn't give anyone else a chance to show their voice.

My friend got baptized in the Holy Spirit!

The preacher lady then preached on the gift of tongues and on the churches being dead in the Holy Spirit...

Then she prayed over people – Wow!

She nailed everyone!

When she got to me – she said – 'You have lots of little things wrong' – and then I was healed!

I started to shake my arms... and she said 'Ok'.

Then I felt her try to push me down and I resisted.

I thought... I am not going to let her push me down.

Then she blew on me – and down I went to the floor!

I curled up into a ball, fetal position, and she spoke these words – 'I come against the spirit of miscommunication in your marriage – where you say one thing and he interprets another and vice-versa. He says black, you say white.'

She was spot on with that!

She broke off ... or rather – delivered the spirit of confusion from our marriage.

I was cringing and wiggling in and out of a ball and weeping furiously.

When she was done, I was able to be flat on my back with my arms stretched out and I kept writhing and moving my legs, but I couldn't get up from the floor.

Then in my head I said, 'I want to get up' because I felt everyone go away and I felt alone.

Then I got up.

I went to Gospel Choir rehearsal and had so much energy and sang like I had never sung before! I was so loud, and the Director kept saying how great the altos were and people in the front row kept turning around to look at me!

I got home and the miscommunication between my husband and I was gone!

Baptized in Water

Easter Monday, April 1, 2002

Weeks before this, I wrote in my journal:

> *I had a dream last night. I saw myself taking off a huge coat of flesh. I was taking off this long coat and my real self underneath was revealed.*

Easter Monday, April 1, 2002

I got baptized in water! The old me was left in the water and I am resurrected with Christ. All things have passed away and I am a new creation in Christ!

The service was short. I helped with the worship.

After the service, we all went downstairs to the pool. We changed. We were about 10-12 being baptized. Two little girls went first. Then a couple from Madagascar.

Then it was my turn.

I got into the pool and it was so cold, freezing. I couldn't get my mind off the cold.

I felt so silent.

The Pastor asked if Jesus was my Lord and Savior and I said, 'Yes!'

The he said, 'In the powerful name of Jesus, I baptize you'

... and then I went backwards into the water.

The minute I hit the water, it was a shock.

I was revived, like my heart stopped beating and then started again – new beginnings.

I felt so alive and restored and filled with so much love. I was so full of love and so happy and content and peaceful on the way home.

My middle daughter got baptized with me.

The Thursday before, she had said the prayer of salvation and she accepted Jesus as her Lord and Savior and was filled with joy. She was jumping around with joy. You could visibly see the change in her. It was special that she wanted to get baptized with me. I hope it was as meaningful an experience for her as it was for me.

Some people came back to the house afterwards and we had a party to celebrate!

I felt this baptism was an act of obedience and a statement that I made.

Now, I can move on.

I did have a very clear vision right when I was going to sleep that night. I could see clearly, but couldn't figure out what it was all about.

I was in a room with stairs on the walls, like bleachers and there were things, not sure what, flying around in suspension, floating. It seemed to me that God was telling me that I was going to start seeing clearer and have visions – the veil of my spirit has been lifted.

January 2003

It was around this time that an American Evangelist, who was living in Wales, came to Paris to my friend's house to speak. I did the worship.

She spoke on Genesis 7:11 and how underneath the ground the great fountains burst forth.

She started to pray for the fire to come down on people. She was spot on with my friends.

She grabbed my hand and started to pray over me about oppression.

The whole time, I kept thinking that I wasn't oppressed, but kept feeling something well up inside of me.

She kept calling it out and calling it out.

It welled up inside me so great that it burst forth in a ROAR!

A very loud ROAR!

And then I roared right in her face.

Since that time, on several occasions, I have felt this intense need to feel the Father's love, like a drug addict going through withdrawals, an intense physical longing for His love – for Yeshua to return.

Both times, they have ended in a cry for Jesus to come back.

This feeling is very intense, my whole body aches for His love ... I can't get enough.

Last week in Domata, my bible school, we prayed the Prayer of Supplication.

I had been having problems with my Mom and I cast her over to the Lord.

I had such a hunger and thirst for the Lord and the presence of Holy Spirit. I just want to be close to the Father. I just want Yeshua to come. I just want to be near Him.

Yesterday, an itinerant minister, Bill, came from Atlanta to Domata, my bible school, as a guest speaker for a week. During the 3rd hour session, he stopped teaching abruptly and called me up front for prayer.

He said, **'I sense the presence of God all over me to anoint you, Bracy, for the future. I impart to you this anointing of God with the laying on of hands. It's the due season for Bracy ... right now.'**

He laid hands on me and I fell out onto the floor under the power of Yahweh. I lay on the floor and I started twitching. The power of Holy Spirit was very strong in the room ... so strong that Bill couldn't continue teaching.

He said, 'The 3rd person of the Trinity is strong in this room. I'd like to take all of you and go out in the streets and cast out demons and heal the sick.'

He tries to continue to teach but can't.

I get up from the floor in the front and crawl back to my desk. I am still shaking.

Bill tries to continue again, but still can't ... everyone stands up and starts to worship.

This declaration comes out of my mouth:

I will never quit.

I will fulfill the will of God in my life.

I hear the Lord say, **'It is your due season. It is your time now. You are guaranteed success.'**

I put my heavy head down on my desk and put my scarf over my head. I am still shaking.

God starts to show me some things:

Genesis 15:1 Fear not. I am your Shield; your reward shall be great.

God shows me again the vision where I am on the stage – a big stage in a stadium – I am standing on it with a Bible in my hand and I am speaking. I am the Speaker. The Lord shows me this, then slowly pans the camera out to the people and there are thousands .... Thousands!

I start crying – I am not worthy – I can't do this – How can I do this?

I hear – You are guaranteed success.

I am overwhelmed at the blessings. I see the ancient door open just a little more.

I shook for a long time, like electricity going through me. I was crying and weeping. I was a mess afterwards. It took me a long time to recover – most of the day.

February 2003

From my journal:

A minister from the States came and what a powerfully anointed teacher of the word he is! The first day, I didn't think anything special but on Tuesday, I had such a revelation of redemption that it shook me to my core.

This knowledge of our new glorified bodies, the new earth – coming down from heaven bringing heaven down to us where memories of this life and the hurts and pains here will be forgotten, a distant memory – it will be a place where there is no evil, no trace of sin or evil ... only good ... and that Jesus purchased all of this on the cross. Redemption is complete – everything is paid for!

This changes everything!

As Greg was teaching, I put my hands on my head and kept saying, 'Is this true?" and I started to weep for the truth that was hitting my spirit. I wept all afternoon, then spent the night praising Him for the glorious revelation.

Then Wednesday, we laid hold of the promises of God, as we fell under the *power of the mighty presence of the Holy Spirit.*

Then Thursday, the mighty majestic power of God showed up as Greg was teaching. As he was speaking, the anointing came upon him and his voice became God's voice.

It was so loud that I could not bear to listen to what he was saying.

It was so powerful that my head immediately dropped on to my book on my desk like a dead weight and I started to tremble.

I went into a vision, as God started to reveal to me things about Unity in Christ and to keep going … that He would take care of everything.

I was shaking and manifesting at my desk the whole time and even after the class was over.

It was so powerful.

June 22, 2003

From my journal:

So much has happened since the last time I wrote. We have finished with Domata Bible School! We had a graduation ceremony on Thursday, June 19th, and it was lovely.

In the morning, we had breakfast together then went upstairs for a 'laying on of hands' ceremony.

As soon as we had started, my pastor had asked me to help with the worship. Right at the beginning, I started to cry and couldn't sing.

I was so overwhelmed at finishing Domata. Overwhelmed at everything that I had come up against and at what lay ahead of me. I was feeling so unworthy and so inadequate of finishing the task the Lord had in store for me.

I was crying, and the Associate Pastor got up to speak and he said, 'I know there are some of you who feel so inadequate – not up to what the Lord has for you ...'.

I knew it was straight from the Lord. What he said was such an encouragement.

I know the Lord is listening to me.

I don't remember all that he said, but it was nice to put words to what I was feeling because I couldn't really tell why I was crying, but I knew it was some kind of being overwhelmed by what the Lord has in store for me.

We then came forward and the Pastor started to lay hands on us.

My neck was twitching like mad, and I was so excited, and my heart was pounding.

I knew the Lord was going to speak to me.

The Pastor came up and laid his hands on me. I fell to my knees and then fell forward ... and then Jesus started to speak ...

He said ... 'Don't worry; I will always be by your side. I will be there with you whatever you need – all you have to do is come up and ask – for peace, for joy, for anything that you need, I will be here ready to give it to you. Don't worry Precious Child, I will be right by your side. I will give you all that you need ... just come up and ask of me.'

I laid on the ground for some time – I wanted His presence to last forever ...

(a little side note) ...

The Sunday before our graduation on June 15th, Unity in Christ had a worship night. It was our first time in Boulogne in the Salle Polyvalente. It was such a nice room. We will be doing many worship evenings there. I really like this room. It is big enough, but not too big and the stage is nice and roomy.

There weren't many people at the worship gathering. There were some people who had walked in off the street. We played a little and it was cooking. The anointing was getting heavy. Several people had words. It was a pleasant evening.

After we finished and we were taking down the equipment, we found gold particles on some of our equipment and on the stage!

Glory!!

We tried to figure out where it had come from.

Did someone have a children's party or something and left behind a bunch of confetti?

We asked the janitor, and he didn't know and between us all, we figured out that it must be God. No one had ever heard of gold dust before. I hadn't, but we knew it was a miracle. Even the janitor was amazed!

(and another side note ...)

Simon Potter came to my church in March and taught on the end times and what to expect.

He said, 'Be patient'.

I had been wondering about my church and if I was in the right place or not.

He did a Wednesday night service and when he came to me in the prayer line, he said, 'Oh you, you are in the right place at the right time – stay where you are.'

(I did not know this man).

Continuing with my journal entry...

In the meantime, we had another worship evening at St Mark's church in Versailles on March 30th. It was wild. Some of the people had just been to a conference where there were people getting healed, people taking their hearing aids out, a man in a wheelchair standing up and walking, another person's eye restored ...

They came to our worship evening ready to give thanks.

I was standing by my middle daughter explaining the overheads and from the first strum of the guitar – the anointing fell ... on us ... on the whole room - heavy like a garment.

Wow!

I felt like superwoman! And I was singing! I don't know who was singing out of my mouth! It sounded like all of heaven came down to play with us that night! It was fantastic! We have never played like that before!

His Fragrance

From my journal:

Unity in Christ met last week on January 20th to pray. My friend and I arrived half an hour early. Another friend started to light the candles before everyone arrived and was having a hard time doing this.

After all the candles were lit, there was such a fragrance, an aroma, in the air. It was so sweet.

I started to get a little light-headed from the fragrance. I could feel a wooing, like pulling me into someplace full of sweetness, pulling me up into the heavens and I went into a vision.

Jesus took my hand and took me to Yahweh and sat me in His lap.

Abba then took me inside of Himself and allowed me to see through His eyes how He sees me.

I could smell the aroma in the house and it smelled just like my friend's house back in Vancouver, Washington. It was the aroma that was transporting me into activation.

It brought back all those memories of how I first came to her house. I was so angry, rebellious, and lost. There was so much power in our prayer times together in her house. The Lord did so much in my life at that time, so much.

This fragrance carried me away into the Spirit, into a trance.

I sat there for a long time, not able to speak.

People started to arrive. I was fixated in this trance-like state. I wanted to stay in this place. I didn't want to miss this time in the Lord's presence.

I was missing my friend and these moments back in Vancouver so much.

My heart was homesick.

I sat there and I couldn't speak. It was hard to hear what people were saying. I couldn't interact with them and my head was so heavy that I had to rest it on the back of the chair.

The Lord transported me back to my friend's house in Vancouver.

I was there.

I smelled it.

I was weeping with the intensity of it all. The love that was shared when we would meet. It was such an extraordinary time.

I could feel her house and the peacefulness there. A deep Shalom came over my whole being. I could feel all the love that had been lavished on me there. All the learning, all the encounters and supernatural experiences that I had there all came flooding back into my mind.

The Lord was showing me and making me 'feel' how He saw me, like you would sit on God's lap and go inside Him and see and feel what He feels for you.

There was such love, so much, so intense.

He showed me how He has loved me from the start, even before I was born.

He showed me how His eyes look at me.

I was out for over an hour.

I was out of it before everyone showed up and I was supposed to be facilitating the prayer. I have never been in such a place before.

It was so powerful and did something to my heart. Even in my sin and weakness, He saw me with a love eternal. His eyes were burning with desire for me.

The night with the Evangelist

March 28th, 2004

Journal entry:

UiC (Unity in Christ) has been having regular invitations since September. We frequently go into Stephen's church in La Courneuve (in France). We made contact with Pastor Ok and Joy in Bobigny. This man has a prophet anointing.

In November, we did a big conference with an Evangelist from the States who was living in England at the time.

This was a very hard learning experience for me and for us as a ministry.

The first night of the conference, the Lord had given me parts of three scriptures in Psalms.

Holy Spirit asked me to sing them.

Just sing them out.

Just sing out the scriptures.

(This was before all the IHOP spontaneous singing of prayers and scripture. No one was doing this or had heard of doing this before.)

I thought and prayed about this. I called my guitar player and told him what Holy Spirit was telling me, and we decided to just do it. He was all in.

It was a very scary thing, because Holy Spirit was asking me to sing these scriptures out without music, just me, in front of a lot of people at the conference.

Obedience is my pathway.

That night, my guitar player started to strum his guitar and I launched into a song, singing the Psalms, the scriptures, the Lord had given me.

(The Lord was showing us the power of the Tehillah. I didn't know what that was at the time.)

(The Tehillah – a song or a hymn of Praise. Spontaneous expression of a spiritual song. It's the only one of the seven Hebrew words of Praise that God inhabits. Ray Hughes)

It was powerful.

The weight of Holy Spirit was tangible.

My friend said she was healed emotionally of something the Lord brought to mind that she didn't even know she had a problem with.

Another friend had an open vision of a chariot coming out of the sky to pick her up.

Another girl said the Lord had given her the exact same scriptures that afternoon.

Synchronization was evident everywhere.

The next night of the conference, Thursday, the Lord was going to really lead us into prophetic spontaneous Tehila worship, as we sang scripture. I was so nervous and a little bit scared, but excited at the new thing God was going to do and do publicly.

Fifteen minutes after we started worship, we got cut off ... totally shut down.

The Evangelist came up on the stage and took over my microphone and she started to sing, herself.

She eventually took over and brought in her own keyboard player so that she could sing.

It was such an awkward time, as we didn't know or understand about how people can hijack things in the spirit and shut them down.

We were too innocent and nice and let it happen.

It was a very hard moment and we all learned some very important lessons.

UiC had provided the whole setup. We had reserved the building. All the equipment was ours. We set everything up. We organized everything and then got shut down to where we couldn't move.

Holy Spirit was grieved.

The Evangelist had an agenda for these nights.

She used us and brought in a 'prophet', but the guy she brought in was not a prophet.

They preached for over 30 minutes on giving and sowing into their ministries.

It was a hard weekend, hard lesson to learn.

To say the least my relationship with the Evangelist was very strained and UIC did not do anything with her again.

(It is hard when you collaborate with someone who has a 'Name' and they come in and do that. We were no one really and just got railroaded, hijacked in the Spirit. We didn't know any better.)

There was so much control and manipulation going on. Each night the offering was way overdone, asking for money.

The Prophet's wife ended up doing worship that last night for the ministering time.

I guess that Evangelist needed a certain kind of style to minister, I don't know.

It was awful.

We were all really hurt.

I thought we would talk about it all, but to this day, it has never been mentioned and on her website, it was mentioned that this was a great meeting.

Lord, help me to understand.

Learning to withstand criticism

Saturday, May 15ᵗʰ, 2004

We went to a church in Trappes, France for their Saturday night 'Diner Gospel'. We arrived and set up, no problem. The Pastor wasn't there, but showed up around 7pm.

Everything was agitated, and you could feel the resistance in the spirit to us being there.

We went into prayer.

We were praying and this joy was coming all over me. I could feel Holy Spirit and the anointing coming strong. We went in to start the worship and we ended up finishing at 2am!

Holy Spirit came down heavy like a spaceship landing. You could hear the loud sound, as if it was shaking the building. It was powerful!

As I launched into singing in tongues, I could feel the heat in the room rising, as if coming from the underthrust of the rocket.

The night was so anointed.

We were so blessed. I hope we were a blessing to those who were there.

On May 2ⁿᵈ, we had a worship night in the Salle Polyvalente in Boulogne.

It was harder.

There were some friends who joined us to teach on prophetic dancing.

We started out instrumental in the spirit.

It was anointed.

We went into the first song, and we were just off.

It was hard.

I had such nice things said to me that night from various people, but I could see my Pastor was uneasy. I felt like she was wanting to speak to me, to criticize what we were doing.

I was pleased because the Lord was with us and those who came to worship understood the evening.

Sure enough, my Pastor came over to speak to me.

Luckily, the Lord had been teaching me to only listen to His voice and not the voice of others.

Someone in my church had warned me about my Pastor, but I was so young in the Lord and naïve.

My Pastor came up to me and said, 'I want to encourage you, but it all felt like a concert. It was too loud, and it looked like you were enjoying being in the spotlight. The Lord spoke to me and said what you're doing is a good thing.'

I said, 'I know it is a good thing.'

As she walked away, I thought ... Shame on you.

I could feel her comments not coming from a good heart.

The Lord protected my heart that night.

The Lord is leading me to be cautious in all that is happening. To only do what He says. Go where He says to go and to not listen to others and their opinions. To be obedient, even if it goes against what others say.

The Lord's voice is very strong right now – saying –

'Be obedient! Listen only to my voice – not the voice of anyone else, but follow my leading and not others, only listen to my voice and do what I want you to do. You might be alone, but you must be obedient to my voice – only!'

There will be people in your walk with God that will not understand what He is leading you to do, what He is asking you to do. We all must learn to follow His voice and to withstand any criticisms with love.

We need to trust the Lord enough in each other that when someone tells me something - (the Lord told me to do this) - that I must trust His work in them and bless them in their obedience.

Looking back –

I wrote this 2/4/2018 in my journal after much healing:

All the Leaders in my life have not been for me. I've spent a lot of time with people who have belittled me and undervalued me, called me names, and tried to put me in a box.

I call it 'cutting the edges off my personality', like I was too much for them. Too intense, rattling cages I wasn't supposed to, asking questions that were better left alone.

The patterns of dysfunction started to unravel in 2011 and maybe even before that.

I wasn't valuing myself, so I was getting what I was projecting.

When the patterns of dysfunction started to unravel and the chains of bondage started to loosen, I learned to set my boundaries in place to get some fresh air.

The impact was explosive.

It felt so right and so good, but everyone around me, where I was setting boundaries, were getting really pissed off at me.

The rage of the inferno coming at me was shielded by my desire to become whole, to walk in my destiny and walk out what I was called to do.

I had a backlog of dreams to fulfill that I had put on the back burner that needed a flame of fire set to them again.

I would encourage everyone to read the Boundaries book and read it often to refresh.

(Boundaries: When to say YES, When to say NO, to take control of your life by John Townsend and Henry Cloud)

August 22nd, 2004
Vancouver Vineyard

My last Sunday in Vancouver on our home visit, I was supposed to go to the Albany Vineyard church and visit some friends. I was so exhausted that I couldn't make the drive.

So, I went to the Vancouver Vineyard. I walked in and Holy Spirit told me that the Associate Pastor was to lay hands on me and that he had something to impart to me. Holy Spirit gave me his actual name.

The worship was anointed that morning and I needed some refreshing. I was very weary.

The Associate Pastor preached on 2 Chronicles, where God fights the battles and all they have to do is stay and wait and be patient. The message hit its mark.

I went up for prayer.

I am praising God because He is going to fight my battles for me.

HALLELUJAH!!

All I have to do is surrender it all up.

Somehow, the girl standing next to me in line up front was holding my hand and there was a lady in front of me trying to ask me some questions about prayer.

I was singing and just having church all by myself. I didn't care what people thought. I needed to take something back with me to Paris.

I felt someone come up behind me to catch me because I could feel that I wasn't going to stay up long.

I stayed up for a long time singing then fell out under the power of God with no one touching me.

God's love fills me up.

When I opened my eyes, there was my French friend huddled over me. She was weeping and just kept saying, 'that was so beautiful and everyone around you was blessed'.

I make my way and sit in a pew right in front.

I am out of it.

I'm thinking the Associate Pastor is going to pray over me, that Holy Spirit will lead him to do that.

Well, he doesn't.

He prays over a couple of people, and I am thinking, '*This is almost over. I am going to have to ask him to pray over me. I am certainly not leaving because I know Holy Spirit has something for me. I just have to ask for it, which is not easy for me.*' I don't want to bother him, but Holy Spirit urges me to go up to him.

I approach him and say, 'God told me you are supposed to pray over me, that you have something to impart to me'.

He stops, reflects for a moment and then says, 'Let's do it.'

The Associate Pastor is a very big man, like a linebacker, but a big kitty cat on the inside. He starts to pray in tongues, and I know he has something from the Lord.

He then says, 'Yes, yes, yes.'

The air fills with electricity.

He says, 'I see a Pony Express and it is coming towards you.'

The anointing is so strong that I can barely stand up.

I can see this chariot coming towards me, flying in the air towards me. It lands right in front of me and there is a red carpet that appears right up to me.

He says, 'Someone is getting out. A messenger. He has a message.'

And I say, 'A message from the King'.

He says, 'Yes, yes!'

He paints a picture of this person all dressed in regal attire. He is getting out of the chariot and coming down the steps towards me and taking out a scroll.

I try to stay up, but the power of the message is too great.

The messenger starts to unroll a scroll. It goes on and on and on.

I am waiting for him to tell me what is written on it and Holy Spirit reveals to me what is written on the scroll.

It is all about **UNITY** of the Body of Christ and oneness in Jesus.

I know this message.

It is written on my heart.

It is a part of me.

It's in my DNA.

It is my message.

There are no words spoken, but the depth of the revelation is great.

I can see Holy Spirit writing with a big pen de plume and royal ink.

The message is heavy, weighted.

Something that was imprinted on my heart and in my DNA before I was born. It is ancient and written before the foundations of the world and written on my heart when He formed me in the womb of my mother.

I immediately know all of this.

The Pastor says, 'You are like Jeremiah – fire stored up in your bones.'

I have had this prophesied over me before.

He continues, 'This message will consume you. You will not only be the message, but the message will become you.'

I fall on the floor, and I feel all these people praying in tongues over me and all around me.

He prays some other things and then another guy to my left starts to have a vision of a horse, white, mighty, majestic, bold, swift, fit for war. This horse is awesome and ready for battle.

This whole time, my mouth is saying, 'Yes Yes Yes.' I am weeping heavily.

I can see it.

I can see it, but my mind is rebelling and not understanding anything at all.

I can see it all.

I am riding on this horse and people are being drawn to this horse.

He says, 'People will be drawn to this. They will come.'

My stomach area starts to hurt and jerk a little and I hear him say,

'Come forth!'

I started to have contractions on the floor, like when you are with child and in labor, heavy, hard, breathing.

He is calling forth things for me and my purpose on this earth and for Unity in Christ ministry and what we need.

I am not sure what these things are, but it is powerful, and I know I need them.

I can't hear him and what he is saying because my stomach area is just contracting like mad and I am writhing on the floor with all these people around me praying and loving on me with words and caresses, like a labor coach when you have a baby.

He prays off the fear of man completely.

(This is something we all need to rid ourselves of completely!!! That people pleasing spirit.)

I have been delivered of this before, but when he said it completely, I knew he meant that I was to have no fear whatsoever at all about what God tells me to do before any man or anyone!!

He puts his fingers on the palm of my right hand and starts calling forth miracles in my ministry.

I am still birthing.

He puts his finger in my vein, like he is giving me a shot, and electricity goes through my body.

All of this is with my eyes closed and I am still contracting and bringing forth.

After the waves dissipate, I hear this little voice say, 'Is she having a baby?'

Finally, we are finished.

I look up and my friend's husband has my youngest daughter in his arms, who is looking at her Momie on the floor and he is explaining what Jesus is doing.

Wow!

Testimony after this encounter from my journal:

October 6th, 2004

Unity in Christ is just getting so blessed. We are doing so many things. We have already had a worship night at St Marks and helped with their Sunday service, done a weekend anniversary at another church, plus Saturday/Sunday rehearsals. We have many people wanting to help financially.

Jesus House just bought all this equipment for us to use, 8000 euros worth and gave us 300euros in the offering.

St Marks has offered to help us out financially.

Jesus House has told us they will buy us anything we need!

PROVISION!

Jehovah Jireh – You are the God of provision!

Sunday, we are back at St Marks and then next Thursday, we have a worship night in our new place with the new equipment.

God is blessing us so.

Changing churches and
the flute player

November 2004

In the Fall of 2004, I left my church where I went to bible school and started to go to another church, a much smaller one. The Lord was very specific in His dealings with me on this.

Holy Spirit had told me to pull away from doing the worship the year before and I didn't listen.

In the Spring, I had tried to pull away from doing so much worship, but it was impossible. I was getting burnt out and needed a rest from doing so much.

I had started to think about this new church when the Elijah list came to Paris for a conference. This new church was the one who had organized the conference and I wanted to be in that church.

I set my heart's intention.

The Lord gave me a dream about my new Pastor. She came to me so clearly in my dream, with her white hair.

She was glowing.

Standing right in front of me, I looked in her eyes and I knew I was to go to her church. The Lord showed me her eyes and how she had wisdom and healing for me.

At the time, I was doing a 37-day prayer focus that Chuck Pierce had put out about refining your vision. There was to be a conference this one weekend with an Evangelist and a Minister from Oregon who ministers using flutes. They were doing the conference together. It was a powerful time for me.

I went to the afternoon session of the conference with the flute player.

Right at the start, when she started to play her flute, I heard actual words, the interpretation, to her melodies, as clear as could be.

I started to sing the words to what she was playing.

I could feel the anointing in the air.

That Thursday night of the conference, the Evangelist called me out and asked me to stand up in front of everyone.

I stood up.

She said, 'There is an open heaven over you. This is your breakthrough Bracy!'

... and I fell out under the power of Holy Spirit right there in my chair!

The next thing I know, the room went wild.

My friend climbed over me to go to the front.

The Glory was dripping like oil in the air.

The next day of the conference, I couldn't wait for my house to be empty. I waited for my husband to go to work and took the kids to school.

I worshiped wildly and ended up on my face on the floor.

I had a vision of the Lord taking my spirit out of my current church, out of the Pastor's hands, and putting it into my new Pastor's hands.

It was very weird!

The Lord told me to go back to the conference that night and I would get confirmation from my new Pastor.

So, I went, and my new pastor, who was hosting the conference, stands up after the anointed worship and says, 'Holy Spirit is leading me to share something.'

I knew it was for me.

She said, 'I normally don't say this' ... but she started to talk about people with ministries – the relationship between people and how they have to be nurtured and held up – lifted up in their ministries – encouraged and not discouraged – helped and not hindered.

I knew this was for me!

The Lord was right, and He is faithful and good!

(In the church that I was in, I was not supported. They couldn't see me in the spirit of who I really was. They accused me of many things, called me into their office and behind my back called me names and slandered my name and what we were doing in Unity in Christ.)

The Lord instructed me to go back for the concert the flute player was giving that Saturday afternoon.

I felt it would be closure for me.

I went with two friends, and I was telling them all that had happened in the car on the way there ... about changing churches, the dream, the vision.

I felt like the Lord was killing me at the time with all that was going on. It was all so overwhelming.

My current Pastor was making a big fuss about UIC and us going and playing at another church on Sunday. He said that I had lied to him and was trying to steal musicians from the church.

It was awful because I had made sure that worship at the church was covered. I had spent time making sure of that.

Thank God I had a mentor in the States who helped me through that very tough moment.

What the Pastor didn't know is that I had his back and had orchestrated and organized everything for that Sunday morning service.

So, that night, at the flute player's concert, I sit down in 'the chair' that she has placed in the front for ministering to people.

For me, she chooses A minor.

Somehow, I KNOW this is my favorite key.

The key A minor is for me and my DNA and frequency.

I KNOW this!

She starts to play over me, and it is like Holy Spirit is playing a melody straight from heaven just for me.

It is so beautiful.

Then she starts to prophesy and sing over me...

'*I see the Lord weeping over you. I see the Lord weeping with you. You feel like you have died 1000 deaths. He knows the rejection, rejection from major relationships in your life. He knows your pain. He sees your scars and wounds and He is massaging those scars. We have to die so we can have more of Him. We go through resurrection/death many times in waves that take us closer to Him, but now the Lord's Glory is on you, and He is rejoicing over you*'.

It was amazing what she sang over me.

How could she know all of that?

It was the Lord.

I felt completely healed of so many things that were happening at the time.

I knew then I was to leave my church and go to Eau Vive.

The Lord was healing me and protecting me.

That day, that Friday, when I was on the floor in my house in Paris receiving revelation about changing churches, in the midst of His presence enveloping me, I had a major revelation about my past, a part of my past that was very difficult for me when we moved from Florida to Tacoma, Washington, right after I graduated from high school.

I realized how I had been totally abandoned, left alone, to fend for myself, at a time that I needed my parents the most. All the things that had happened to me, the bad decisions that I made and how they had devastated me and showed me how totally alone I was, rejected and abandoned by my parents, as they were fighting for their marriage. They had big issues they were dealing with and ended up getting a divorce, which devastated me completely.

Divorce is devastating, no matter what your age. I was a young adult and I needed guidance from my parents at a very important phase of my life, and they both were not able to give me anything because they were dealing with their own stuff.

I realized, in that moment, that it wasn't my fault – the circumstances – and I wept so hard that there was a huge puddle of tears on the floor.

It hurt so much to know how alone I was and all my bad decisions and mistakes ... but the Lord was right there with me, beside me.

I cried and cried and cried.

Then that weird Spirit thing happened where God took my spirit out of me and put it into the hands of my new Pastor.

So, I left my church.

I made an appointment to meet with the Pastor and Associate

Pastor.

I had agreed to do the worship for the whole upcoming conference ... and I did.

I was faithful to my commitment.

Then Holy Spirit lifted the grace for me to be there and I couldn't sing anymore.

That was my last Sunday there.

On my way – before I left the house – to go speak with them, I went into the bathroom of my house and a spirit of doubt fell on me hard. I was fasting that day to be prepared and alert.

The Lord brought to mind all that He had shown me – the dream, the vision and all the confirmations – otherwise, I might not have left the house.

In the car on the way there, I started to think back on all that I had learned there in that church.

I came there not even raising my hands, knowing nothing about the spiritual realm, just a baby.

How far I had come and the opportunity to lead worship and Domata (Rhema Bible school for missionaries in the field) and all that I had learned there – all the spiritual growth that I had there – and I started to cry.

I started to release gratitude to my Pastor and Associate Pastor.

So, when I got to the church, I was in an attitude of gratitude.

My Pastor and Associate Pastor had no idea what I was going to say.

I started off by thanking them for everything and I got caught up in my throat trying to get the words out.

I started to cry, a deep cry that came from deep down inside of me.

It caught me by surprise.

I then told them that I was leaving, and they were silent.

I left with their blessing over me and my family.

Minister from the desert with the hot sauce

This minister came to my church the 2nd week of March. I believe it was 2004. He was there 3 nights and then we – Unity in Christ - were with him, doing worship Thursday night at Evy's place in Trappes, France.

The first night was mainly about healing – many were healed. He is a great Teacher and a true Prophet.

Tuesday night was all prophecy. He prophesied over me ...

He said, 'the Lord is getting ready to take you from baby steps to taking big steps. The Lord has heard your cries and He is getting ready to answer your prayers.'

I had just been out on a morning walk with my dog, and I was crying out to God because He was showing me how I had to go alone where He was taking me, that I can't take anyone with me.

It is my walk.

I wanted others to come with me, but it is not for them.

It is my walk.

I was feeling alone, like I was being pushed out to the front, with my hands holding onto other people. My hands were being pried out of their hands and the Lord was pushing me out to the front – in front.

I was crying out for the Lord to send me the true worshippers.

I was weeping at God pushing me forward.

I felt so alone at having to leave people behind and scared at being alone in front, a forerunner.

He told me He was right there beside me.

Praise God!

The Lord was lifting something from me, cracking my outer shell, like a pomegranate fruit being turned inside out and showing/revealing its vulnerable fruit inside for anyone to see.

Wednesday night was so great. I had taken a friend with me. She actually got healed from debilitating migraines. It had plagued her most of her life.

Thursday night at Evy's. There was so much warfare to even get there.

It was in this old building with some of the windows smashed out.

The elevator was broken, and we had to haul all our gear up 5 flights of stairs.

The room was electric.

Evy's church had done an Esther fast, only bread and water, for three days before we came, and you could feel the hunger and tension of the presence of God in the room.

It was a bit chaotic getting everything set up. It took us 2 hours to get set up.

Evy spoke for a bit, and we started the worship after she got up and prayed.

It was so anointed.

The room was hopping.

Everyone was up and clapping, singing so loud.

It was wonderful and amazing.

Right as we were starting, even before that, people stood up and were going crazy.

I felt this vibration in the Spirit, like a space rocket booster starting up.

It was powerful.

The Glory of God was in the room.

We worshiped and then before you knew it, it was 1:00am in the morning!

The disappearing time thing again.

From my journal:

I am feeling like I have been promoted to another level in the Spirit. I can sense Holy Spirit so clearly and strongly. It is wonderful ... so strong, but I also feel so vulnerable, softer, like my harder edge is gone. I feel more compassion. I find myself listening more intently and feeling such a deep peace – a knowing deep down that God is there walking beside me – near me.

Lord – help me to follow you no matter what other people say.

Help me Lord to be obedient to your calling and Your voice.

Help me to hear You and act when You speak.

Lord Jesus, I love You so much that sometimes it hurts me how much I long for You.

I am desperate for You, Lord.

Oh yeah ... the hot sauce. This minister used to bring his own hot sauce to France and when we would go out to eat, he would put that hot sauce all over his lovely French food. Never understood that.

March 2004

From my journal:

The thing is .... Since they have left (these were members of UiC), we have been having unbelievable times of worship and rehearsal times.

Many times, as we launch into singing scripture – we have heard choruses of Angels and the real manifest presence of the Lord among us.

The Lord is leading us into the Spirit – into intercession in worship – into prophecy in worship.

We go off in the Spirit and heaven comes down to us – to meet with us.

It is wonderful, the places we go together in the Spirit.

The Lord will bring alignment. He will send people away and bring people to you. It is His order and timing. We need to be aware of this so we can bless those who move on to fulfill what God is calling them to and receive with honor those who join us.

Kathy Walters prophecy
June 5th, 2004

Someone had orchestrated and brought Kathy Walters to Paris.

There was a conference and the Lord had told me to go to it. He said that Kathy had something for me.

So, I went with some friends on the Friday night of the conference.

It was good.

She announced that she was going to pray for people the next morning and not to miss out.

At that time, I was very constrained in my marriage and couldn't really see any way of going the next day, but I felt a deep urging inside me to GO!

I told my husband that I was going to go back to the conference with a friend the next day.

I went outside the next morning to leave and my car wouldn't start.

It seems an animal had chewed through some pipes close to the engine making it impossible to start the car.

I was furious.

I called my friend in a panic and she swung by and picked me up.

I was all jacked up because I knew Kathy had something for me.

We all got there and found our seats.

She preached and then asked everyone to come up front who wanted prayer.

That was everyone in the room.

She wanted to pray against the 'not-qualifying' spirit and the spirit of doubt.

The Lord had told me to go the minute I found out she was coming to Paris, so my heart was in a super expectant posture. The Lord told me she was going to give me an impartation in the spirit.

There was such an anointing when she was praying.

There was a long line of people, and she was going down the line, praying for everyone. People were just falling out by the power of His presence, one by one. Everyone.

She came to the girl standing next to me.

The weight of God's presence was so strong, I could barely stand up.

As she was praying for the girl, I was receiving what she was speaking over her. I could feel her pull out arrows and darts of negative comments out of her back... and out of mine too.

Kathy came up to me and stood right in front of me. The anointing was strong. I wanted to stay standing so she would prophecy over me. A lot of times when you fall out, preachers just walk on by ... but I had come for something today.

She put her hands over my ears and prayed out the religious spirit

– the things you hear and receive in churches from just being there.

I was manifesting hard now, crying, shaking, and trembling under the mighty power of God's hand on my life.

She prayed for impartation.

I felt her lift my hands up in the air and at that moment I grabbed hold of her hands.

I interlocked my fingers with hers and held on tight.

I heard her say – 'she is doing something to my fingers'.

I clenched down hard on her hands. I did not want to leave that place without receiving what I had come for.

The minute I grabbed her hands, I felt electricity go through my hands and down my arms. I couldn't let go and I fell out under the power of God and pulled Kathy down with me, right on top of me.

She untangled from me and came over the top of me and broke off, cut off, a crippling spirit.

The crippling spirit that is hindering and crippling my anointing.

(The thought went through my head. What does this mean?)

She prayed off every and all negative words spoken over me.

She called forth the 'SEER' anointing in me.

(At that time, no one knew what the SEER gifting was, and I was lying on the floor arguing with the Lord about how I didn't know what that was and that I wasn't sure that I wanted that.)

On the floor, I was feeling electricity going through my whole body.

God was changing some things! This I knew! It was so powerful, it was rocking my whole being.

At that moment, I entered into a vision.

I had a vision of Jesus standing up, looking right at me.

Then He knelt down in front of a trough full of water. He was putting His hands in it and telling me to come and drink.

He said, 'Come drink, come and drink, precious child'.

Jesus then put the cup to my lips.

It was Wisdom's cup (Proverbs 2) and I drank and drank.

He was revealing to me that things would be different from today.

He was changing all of that.

He told me He was going to change everything today.

Now!

He told me I would get great impartation from Kathy... to get ready.

He was joyful, giggling, happy, and had a gleam in His eyes.

I saw Jesus then standing over me.

He was glorious!

He was saying He was increasing my anointing.

He said, 'I am increasing you! I am giving you more and more.'

He told me to come with Him.

I could see Him on top of a mountain overlooking a rich, lush valley.

He said, 'Get on my back and fly with me, fly like an eagle' and we took off.

I don't know how long I was on the floor, but I was certain I wasn't getting up until Holy Spirit was finished with me.

Kathy Walters article in the Elijah List

January 6th, 2005

I was sitting at my desk at my home in Bailly, France, reading an article posted by Kathy Walters on the Elijah List, talking about walking in our inheritance, walking in the Spirit every day and what that should look like. She said that supernatural encounters and experiences, miracles, signs and wonders should be normal everyday occurrences for believers.

This revelation of supernatural manifestations being normal was really touching me deep. Holy Spirit was very present in this moment, and I could feel Him there with me, right by my side, wanting to show me something, wanting to teach me something.

I got to the point where Kathy says, '... and you need to think how God thinks.'

I read that statement over and over and over and over ...

... and I realized how much doubt I had about UiC and the Lord coming through on all the visions He had given me and all the things He had shown me and all my encounters ...

... and I started to repent.

I started to weep.

I shouted out loud ... 'Lord show me what is behind Unity in Christ! I need to know!!!'

... and immediately I was taken up in the spirit into heaven and I saw this HUGE, ENORMOUS – bigger than life – I saw this dark gray cloud – HUGE – with a Mr. North Wind face getting ready to blow – and Holy Spirit said, 'This is what is behind UiC'.

The power in that dark cloud was so strong, so powerful, more than I had ever felt before.

I could feel the immense authority in its form.

It was so great that the minute the dark cloud started to blow, I got frightened and I 'came back down' into myself at my desk.

I sat there a moment, frightened by the power I had just seen and experienced and started to doubt what I had just seen and experienced.

Was that God?

Was that the enemy?

Can that kind of power be God?

It was terrifying.

Holy Spirit wasn't finished with me yet and I started crying, weeping and trembling.

I put my hands out in front of me, arms stretched out on my desk, palms up in the air.

I felt Jesus take them and lay them down on the desk and impart power and authority into my hands.

I was shaking the whole time.

It was one of the most powerful things I have ever felt in my life.

It took me some time to come out of that experience.

The Lord was showing me the immense power and authority that is found in Him. The vastness of that dark cloud and the power pulsating with the fear of the Lord was indescribable and it scared me awake.

He was showing me our power and authority that we have in HIM.

January 1, 2006
Back in the States

From my journal:

This is definitely a NEW SEASON in the Lord.

For about 2 months now, the Lord has had me in complete rest.

At first, it was very hard, as I couldn't turn off my mind from creating and putting things together.

He then gave me a vision:

I saw Jesus carrying me up a long flight of stairs. I was in a lovely, beautiful flowing gown that was glowing with light and there was a glory light all around us. He was carrying me up the stairs to Father. I was completely limp in His arms, head back, arms stretched out.

I was beautiful, but I looked fatigued and weary, battle weary, with wounds and scars all over my body.

I was having this vision, as I was crying out to the Lord, how I didn't know how to rest. I was asking Him how to rest, that I didn't know how.

After the vision, I felt Him put His hand on my chest and I felt such a warmth and peace flow into me. I felt Him healing me from the last 3 years in ministry in Unity in Christ.

I have needed rest. Looking back at all the struggles of the last year. Ministry is hard.

I believe ministry should not look like this. Our relationships were empty. People in ministry should be close, like living stones knitted together.

I miss it dearly, but am glad to be free of the bad part of it, the struggling, the aloneness as a forerunner. The misunderstandings, the spiritual battles. I am so grateful for all the Lord has done through us, but glad that it is finished.

March 2006 – Injected with Glory

From my journal:

Today, I went to a friend's house, here in Vancouver, to chat and have some lunch. We had a bite to eat. Then we went into the living room to chat. We were just catching up and having a nice time together.

Suddenly, my friend says ... *WE NEED TO PRAY! NOW!*

We start praying and the air in the room gets heavy, the atmosphere gets heavy.

This anointing – this presence – comes into her living room.

This presence is heavy and pushes us both down into the couch.

It is pushing down every cell in my body into the couch.

It is happening to both of us at the same time.

We looked at each other in astonishment and amazement, asking each other what was going on.

We both understood that this was a divine appointment.

We were not scared or fearful at all.

Her dog rushes into the room and starts spinning in circles around swiftly, chasing its tail.

We start to laugh out loud.

Both of us felt the same exact thing.

It felt as if this presence (I still don't know if it was an angel or a heavenly being or what) was extracting the blood out of my body and then putting in new glory blood of God's divine nature into my body, like we were being injected with a divine nature, like our bodies were taking on divine nature characteristics.

The atmosphere was so heavy with God's presence.

There was no revelation – just visitation.

I believe we got visited!

It felt like God was giving us something – an anointing – for something we are going to need.

It is all so interrelated!

I don't know how long we were like this – but it was strong – 1000x stronger than anything I have ever experienced.

It was bewildering – awesome – amazing.

Then I felt like I was being lifted up into the heavens.

I knew I was being taken to the Throne of God.

As I approached, I couldn't see the throne, but just getting so close and seeing and feeling the rays of His Glory was so intense.

I thought I was going to melt.

His goodness and love, and warmth were so intense. It was hard to stay in this presence without weeping and His strength and love was powerful.

Then something started pushing me faster ahead and everything was going by so fast, like I was in space – in Star Wars – flying 10,000 miles an hour through space.

I still had no revelation and neither did my friend – but I KNOW God gave us something.

It was so intense.

I have never felt anything like it.

LOVE

Love is a very interesting and profound thing. On one hand, it can be so superficial, and on the other, you can never find the depths of it.

Where does it end?

As we pray, Lord, let me see as You see ... let me have eyes to see and ears to hear as You do; as we open our hearts past the woundedness and hurting of our past, into this glorious love, He unfolds to us little by little, showing us just as much as we can handle. We can slowly start to walk as Jesus did.

Without the revelation knowledge of LOVE – we cannot do this.

How easy is it to love someone who loves you back?

Oh, the joy of it!

That two-sided relationship is so rare these days. The love shared between 2 people, 2 friends, in Christ, is so wonderful, such a gift.

But can we withstand love where love is not returned?

Can we face rejection, look at it straight on, and still love, even in the face of undeniable, clear-cut abandonment from another?

Can we still look at them, in the face of emptiness, and still love them in the depths of our heart?

I keep thinking of Jesus on His way to the cross and how, in the face of rejection and reviling, He had eyes to see as the Father sees. He was so close to the Father that nothing they did to him, the spitting and name-calling and hatred and murder ... could even touch Him.

O God ... I want to know this LOVE.

I want to be so close to You that even in the face of rejection and abandonment, I can still LOVE.

Show me, open my eyes.

Open my heart to this Love.

For this is not a natural love, this is not a superficial love, this is not a love that goes away, or we can turn away from and not love another anymore.

No!

This is not possible.

When we have our eyes opened into the supernaturalness of His love, we begin. Yes, we begin to see, just start to get a glimpse, a highlight of this love.

I chose this day to follow this Love.

I chose this day to Love in the place of anything that comes my way.

This is my pursuit.

I can love my friends, my wonderful sisters and brothers in Christ, but can I love those 'friends' where that love is not shown?

Can I love those 'friends' who hurt and wound me with their mouths?

Can I love those who openly disagree with me about You, God?

Can I love those who hate me because of my love for You?

Where does love end?

One thing I do know is that I do not know You or Your ways.

They are too high for me.

Whatever I know of You God is like a grain of sand in comparison to what and who You are.

The fulfillment would certainly crush me ...

Oh God, my heart cries out to You to reveal this LOVE

Jesus, how did You do it?

How?

I want to know this.

I know this comes with a price. Will I be willing to pay it, to lay it all down for LOVE?

One thing I have learned is that we don't know how to have relationships. We don't know how to live and love in truth. We hide, we play games, we speak and don't speak, we merrily go around the mulberry bush living our lives separate from one another.

We see each other and 'talk'. Maybe we get concerned about someone and their life – but do we really walk in love speaking truth?

I have found, as I examine my life, that I don't do this.

It is hard.

I am sitting here writing this in my mother's house in Virginia, as she recovers in a rehabilitation place, recovering from something the Doctors can only explain as dementia from old age. (She was actually having mini strokes that they didn't know about.)

As my mother goes in and out of lucidity, she realizes how she continually said no to the advances of love from her friends trying to spend time with her. They were making an effort and she rejected their efforts. She regrets that time lost now, as she sits in her wheelchair, barely able to move around.

What is deducted from all of this is that Love takes effort, even when you don't want to, you must get past your flesh and spend time and make an effort and love with full force, even if your heart gets broken.

Graham Cooke says he wants to live this way and just learn to heal faster.

What is stopping us from this Love?

Is it fear?

Pride?

Laziness?

Apathy?

God, help us to get past ourselves and learn to Love as You love.

Give us a heart and mind to get past our own flesh, our own selves, our own issues and Love each other, encourage each other, edify each other.

Teach us how to LOVE.

CATALYST

Looking back, taking a bit of time to reflect, everything has gone by so fast these last couple of years, that I am going to spend some time looking back, with gratitude, at all that has happened.

God said I would marvel... and I am marveling, overwhelmed by His goodness and His faithfulness to accomplish what He promised.

I have kept all my emails, and prayer requests throughout the whole journey of the recording of my debut CD ... Him and Me... "Awakened" ... and I want to share some of the journey so that you can be encouraged.

So that you can know and be confident in the gifts and talents that you have and that you must break through any fear that you have and create.

In January of 2011, I was in ministry over at New Heights church in an outreach ministry called Friend2Friend.

I started telling everyone that I was going to record a CD in June.

I was speaking it out loud so that I wouldn't chicken out.

At this point in time, it had been 10 years since I had dreamed and desired to record my original songs straight from His heart to mine.

My friend's daughter had given me a name and number of a guy she was recording with about 18 months before.

I don't know what was holding me back from calling him. What I do know is that it was all about His timing!

Another important part of this journey was that I had spent the last 6 years killing any dream, desire, or ambition that I had of resurrecting anything like the ministry that I had in France, Unity in Christ. I had tried so many times to resurrect it and failed. I chopped and hacked those desires up, buried them deep in the ground several times and let them all die.

It was a continual process of about 7 years. It was so painful. What happened in France was so good, even amongst all the crap.

I knew that a kernel of wheat had to fall to the ground...that it had to die for God to resurrect it into something glorious.

He had to be the one to do it... Him alone.

I gave up what I am called to do.

I gave up singing, leading, for HIM.

I laid it all down seeking only Him and His face.

I said... all I want is you Jesus... and that is what happened.

It was just the two of us, alone, for many years.

During this time of hiddenness, I drove around A LOT helping others in their ministries, going wherever He told me to go and helping whomever He said.

I crossed the bridge into Portland, Oregon so many times, sowing into other people's ministries. I saw this as a prophetic act to link the two cities together, sowing from the north to the south.

This dream and desire were such a part of me that I couldn't even think about it without weeping.

I chose not to think about it ... ever again.

It was too painful.

I was trying to entirely wipe it from my mind, and I was succeeding at it.

In April of 2011, Holy Spirit started to stir up in me the desire again, the desires I had locked up tight in my heart.

Trying my best to suppress this yearning with angry prayers to the Lord of, 'don't stir this up unless you are going to act on it; and don't stir it up before it is time; please don't'.

My emotions were all over the place, as He started to stir up those dreams and desires that I had buried deep down in my heart.

As He was stirring up these old dreams, I wrestled with Him saying... 'Don't tease me! Don't awaken love before its time! DON'T! It is too painful. I can't take one more time!'

I can still feel the emotions as I am writing this, but He kept unlocking those doors, bringing out thoughts and dreams and desires, as I would try to push them back into their respective places in my heart and lock them up again.

In May, there was a conference at Canby Grove.

A friend, an evangelist, from New Zealand was speaking.

The Lord told me to go.

I always love to hear him speak, as he is such a great encouragement to the Northwest.

Reluctantly, I went to Canby Grove that night.

I didn't want to go because it is so far, and no one would go with me.

I went alone.

I had been wrestling with the Lord for about a month on this.

God was moving powerfully in my life, my marriage!

Everything around me was turning into meadows of beautiful flowers and I didn't want to mess it up by bringing out old dreams from the past.

They were dead.

I sat near the front, 2nd row from the front, aisle seat.

There was worship, then my friend spoke.

It was good.

We all stood up and then he started to pray.

One of the first things he did was he came over to me and he laid his hand on my shoulder and said, 'Bracy, it is time to dream those old dreams again, dig up the ancient desires!'

The Power of God hit me, and I fell to the floor!

I couldn't believe it.

How could he know?

He prayed over me for a long time, keeping his hand glued to my head the whole time, calling out ... 'CATALYST! CATALYST! YOU ARE A FIRESTARTER'!

I was on the floor manifesting, crying, weeping, roaring, laughing.

I was the only one in the crowd on the floor making a spectacle of myself, but I didn't care.

The power of God was all over me and I wasn't going to get up until it was over.

I stayed there for a long while, until finally, I called out for help. To help me get up and go to the bathroom, but it was like all the bones had been taken out of my body.

I didn't understand what had just happened.

The Lord hadn't said anything to me while I was on the floor, hadn't revealed anything to me, but I knew it was powerful and that something would come out of it.

I think my heart was in such a state of hiddenness, that the shock of that night bolted me awake.

It reminded me of a time before when I sang on a worship team for the first time while we were living in France back in 2001. I had never been in a charismatic church. Before moving, I attended a Lutheran church. We sang hymns. I didn't know what worship was. This was my second time going to this church. That Sunday, under the heavy leading of Holy Spirit, I went up to the worship leader and said... you need a female singer, and I am it!

I was shocked that I had said that!

He said ... 'Come back to practice on Saturday. You sing on Sunday.'

So, I show up on Sunday. We were singing six or seven songs, all in French ... and I knew only one! We started and immediately the power of God hit me, and I was hanging on the microphone for balance. I could feel a very big angel pouring a large bucket of oil on my head anointing me as a worship leader. I don't know what I did or what I sang... but after that experience, Unity in Christ was born.

So... back to Canby Grove and I am on the floor. The Lord didn't say anything to me the whole time I was on the floor, and I was on the floor a long time, almost until the room had cleared of people.

Nor did He speak for the next 3 days, as I still felt His powerful presence on me.

It felt like a big blanket of power that was covering me.

I knew something was to come out of it.

I was certain!

About a week later, I started to cry out one day in my car. It just burst out of me like a flowing river. I started to speak out loud what it is I am called to do!

I said... 'Papa, I want to sing! I want to record! I want to create! I want a band!

I want to travel and sing and speak and write!

You called me as a Christian singer when I was 16...

You poured buckets of oil on my head anointing me the 1st time I sang on a worship team....

OPEN UP MY DESTINY!

OPEN IT UP NOW!!'

One month later, I was entering Larry's studio to record two songs that ended up in a CD recording of 12 original songs that I had written while living in France.

Out of the speaking of my mouth came forth everything that has happened and is happening.

I was learning how to frame my world, speak the unseen things into the seen realm, how to manifest.

It was overwhelming.

One thing I know is that I had been prepared for it all.

He has prepared me to handle all that was coming my way!

I think there are many in the Body of Christ just like me... waiting .... in fear of failure, in fear of success.

I went into that recording studio that first day, having a panic attack. I was so scared... but I found my destiny and what I was called to do and created for. The wall of fear was so great, it felt like a membrane that I had to push through.

Joyce Meyer posted on Facebook the day I was going to Larry's studio.

I saw it before I left the house.

Her post: You got fear?

DO IT AFRAID!!

So... I did it afraid!

There are so many gifted and talented Christians who have been sitting in their caves, ministering unto the Lord with their songs, with their art, with their creativity, their dreams and desires.... waiting.

And I believe ...

NOW IS THE TIME TO TRY AGAIN!!!

SPEAK OUT WHAT IT IS YOU DESIRE.

WHAT IT IS HE HAS CALLED YOU TO DO!!

YOUR WORDS WILL CREATE YOUR DESTINY....

IT IS THE TIME TO SPEAK OUT YOUR DESTINY!

All the angels and heavenly hosts are waiting for us to SPEAK!!!

...so, they can move...

PART TWO

Conference in
Coeur D'Alene, Idaho

9/25/2014

I was at a conference in Coeur D'Alene, Idaho. During the worship, two large angels showed up on either side of me. Their presence was putting pressure on either side of me to hold me still and in place. I felt a large hand being placed on the front of me and on the back, holding me, bracing me to not move.

A host of angels then showed up all around me and started to work. They were small, tiny, and fairy-like, translucent, but were goldish in color.

Instantly, they started to weave a crown of gold on the top of my head. I could see they were using gold thread to do their work.

I was fixated in my place and couldn't move as the angels worked.

It was a very joyful and pleasant experience, as the worker angels were very happy to be doing what they were doing.

The crown of gold on my head was being created. It was intertwined with blasts of color. They were inserting bursts of light and supernatural galaxies infused with the DNA of heaven.

As they were working, my Cloud of Witnesses* showed up, my Ekklesia in heaven. They were watching the whole process and cheering me on.

More angels showed up and started to work on my chest area. They started to weave my Priestly breastplate, my Ephod, onto my chest. They were creating it out of the same gold thread as they were using for my crown. They left 12 open spots on the breastplate for gemstones to be added.

That day, I received an emerald gemstone and an opal gemstone that was inserted into my breastplate.

The angels holding me in place were firm and I knew I was not to move.

This took the whole time during worship, probably an hour and a half.

*Footnote - Cloud of witnesses

Hebrew 12 – Therefore, since we are surrounded by so great a cloud of witnesses, let us also lay aside every weight, and sin which clings so closely, and let us run with perseverance the race that is set before us, looking to Jesus the pioneer and perfecter of our faith. RSV

Eating of His fruit

This activation encounter occurred as I was meditating on the Song of Solomon.

As I was reading and meditating, Holy Spirit showed up. I could feel His powerful presence all around me, stirring my heart.

Suddenly, supernaturally, the pages of the book of the Song of Solomon 'opened up' in the spirit right in front of me, like a life-like enormous book that was illuminated with a golden hew. The pages became life-like, and I felt an invitation to enter into them.

I found myself delightfully entering the pages of my Bible, entering the words on the page, like walking into a room. It was right in front of my eyes and the pages were opening up and moving to and fro. I found myself going through the words on the page. It was as if I was entering into the Book, walking into the book, as the words floated past me.

As I was in the spirit, I saw a green grassy meadow just ahead of me. The grass was alive and moving. It was Eden.

I walked up a grassy hill and sat down in the shade of a tree and waited.

Peace surrounded me and I felt so good, warmth all around me.

Jesus showed up and walked up the hill and sat down next to me and started to teach me things. He was stroking my brow and my hair. It was very loving and tender.

No words were spoken, just a revelation heart to heart.

Impartation.

Cardiogenesis.

I could feel that I was under His apple tree and eating of His fruit.

He was revealing to me hidden mysteries of who He is and how He is for me.

I could feel ancient knowledge being given to me without speaking.

I sat under that tree for a long while letting Him impart His wisdom to me.

I came out of my encounter and sat down at my piano and wrote this song:

Lyrics:

I sat down in your shade with great delight

His fruit was sweet to my taste

Behold, you are beautiful my Love

Behold, you are beautiful my dove

Truly, you are beautiful

I see dark but you see lovely

I see ashes, but you see beauty for my ashes

October 2020

I had a dinner at my house with my NorthGate team. After we ate dinner together, we went into my living room to worship. I started to play some of the songs I have written since recording my CD. I came upon this song and started to play it. Everyone went into encounter and had amazing visions during the worship. I was astounded at the activation on this song.

January 17th, 2014 – Friday

From my activation journal:

I just had an encounter after a phone call with the Ladies of Gold. Someone at a conference had nicknamed us that. I could feel I needed to sit on my green couch downstairs in the living room.

The Spirit of Council came to get me. I have never met him before. He said he had been waiting for this day to show me the 12 Council chambers.

He switched on my Mantle of Leadership, like a light switch being turned on.

In a flash, I saw in bright colors, a throne with a Lion sitting on it with a purple fur cape, laced with white and black dots on the fringes covering his shoulders and an enormous crown on His head.

The Spirit of Council took my hand and led me down a long hallway. I could feel the reverence and the need to be quiet.

We entered the Council chambers.

I was sitting way down low, looking up at them, observing.

I was quiet.

I thanked him for bringing me.

Then he said, 'They are talking about what you did today with the Ladies of Gold and hammering them into the ground.'

We had had a meeting and at the end of the meeting, as a prophetic gesture, I took a big hammer in the spirit and hammered each one of us into the ground, grounding us into His foundation.

I said to the Spirit of Council that I was too low down and that I couldn't see them.

Then suddenly, the seat that I was sitting on began to rise up and up and up – far above the 12 council members – so they could see me, like a hydraulic lift lifting my chair into the air.

I started to cry with fear and some trembling, being humbled by their majesty and power.

I could only see the Lion the whole time.

His presence reassured me.

He thanked me and said my Leadership Mantle was turned on, that man has not seen this in me, but they all know.

With my chair still up there in the air, I hear a voice tell me to go to the piano and just play – with my eyes closed! Just put your fingers on the keys and start to play.

I do that.

I am amazed at what is happening.

I am playing these beautiful things as my fingers are guided over the piano keys.

(I need to do this more and let the heavenly host direct me.)

I try to go upstairs, but the spirit of Council makes me sit back down on the couch because I am still in the Chambers, and we are not done yet.

I apologize for being immature and not understanding the protocol and I sit down.

Someone says, 'We need to give you your new mantle and crown.'

I stand up and I feel the same purple coat lined with the white and black dots come upon my shoulders and a huge crown placed on my head.

There are cities and nations in my crown – some of them I know, some that I don't know.

I will know when the time is right.

I move forward and I am directed to kneel down on my right knee.

I bow my head and the Lion knights me with a huge blade of a sword on my right shoulder – then my head – then my left shoulder.

I stand up and say thank you.

My chair goes back down, and I am released.

Side note -

We need to be asking for more.

More of Holy Spirit's presence, more visions, more activation in the Spirit, more knowledge and wisdom, more understanding, more strength and to know our authority which is given from our seated place at His right hand in the middle of His name.

January 3rd, 2014
Working on the Gateway
of 1ˢᵗ Love

From my activation journal:

This morning I woke up and I have the whole house to myself, which is rare.

I ascended into heaven and asked Jesus to finally carry me across the threshold of my first love gate.

He said, 'It isn't time yet.'

He took me back to my first love experience.

I ended up forgiving the young man for not seeing me, for not honoring me and not loving me.

For me, it was love at first sight. I was 15 years old, and he crushed my young innocent heart. I fell hard, wept for days. I forgave him and released him.

Then I started forgiving everyone who had rejected me: leaders, friends and everyone else who wasn't able to see me rightly.

Then I said – 'Break off all rejection off my first love gate.'

I then saw a door open up in the spirit.

I took a chisel tool and started chipping away at rejection.

Jesus was in the doorway helping me and I could feel and see the doorway being cleaned of all the chips of rejection falling off as we chipped away at all the rejection attached to my first love gate.

Continuation – January 21st, 2014

Encountering my first love gate again.

Side note:

(We can go back into our encounters, our visions, and activations from the Lord. We can activate them and go back into them and look around and ask questions about why we had the encounter and what was the purpose. It's not just a one and done thing, but the Lord is trying to get our attention through these things and to pay attention to something. There is more meaning that we can discern when we go back and ask Him questions about why this happened and why He showed us what He did.)

In the spirit, I saw an ancient door in front of me.

The minute I showed up in front of the door, the door burst open with the golden, white glory of the Lord and a King came walking through the door and immediately embraced me.

He took me in His arms and embraced me.

My clothes turned from a basic linen dress to royal clothing, a red robe and crown, and we danced intimately.

There was a moment when He turned into a Lion and walked proudly around me.

Then He sat down on my left side.

We went into the King's chambers and embraced and became one.

Side note:

(This was not a sexual thing. Becoming one was like he absorbed me into Him. The particles of my being were intermingled with His and we became one being. I became Him and He became me. Oneness)

Out of that intimacy, the desire to visit Eden came.

He took me, led me, playfully, joyfully, through the two Cherubim with the flaming swords.

It was playful, easy.

We entered Eden.

The grass was huge and alive.

Everything was alive.

I saw that every time I put my foot down, that a pathway was created before me – a golden road in front of me to walk.

I could feel the authority I had over creation.

Lovingly, I would wave my hand, and gold dust would sprinkle everywhere, as I was creating and shifting.

Then Jesus lifted me up and a tree came out of the ground. He picked me up and put me on top of His heights, on the top of the tree, so that I could see.

I could see all of creation and it was alive and clapping and speaking, communicating with me without words.

The Father, Jesus and Holy Spirit surrounded me, embraced me in a huddle and lifted their hands and I came out of that huddle as an orb of light, pure spirit, and they shot me out into the galaxies.

January 9, 2014
Mentoring session

I started watching a mentoring session with a minister and two others on a Zoom call.

He started going in depth about our identity as SONS.

He was talking about the 9 stones, the 9 strands – 3 from Father; 3 from Jesus; 3 from Holy Spirit – added to our 3 strands (our DNA + His light when we are saved); and the 5 stones of fire, intimacy – and the 1st stone is LOVE.

As he stepped onto that first stone, he had an amazing encounter.

As he was describing the encounter, I could feel Wisdom show up on my left side.

I could feel angels all around me.

My cloud of witnesses showed up and I could feel heaven coming upon me, all around me.

I stopped the Zoom call and went into an encounter.

It was a little hazy at first, but I could feel the angels and other heavenly beings all in a flutter...busy...moving around... communicating together.

Then I saw a horse, a white stallion with a long blond mane.

The angels and heavenly beings were pushing me up onto the back of this horse, putting my legs over the back, trying to push me up onto this horse.

I was dead weight.

I didn't know how to get on...

I was listless.

They pushed me up onto this horse and I instantly KNEW that SHE was my horse.

That we knew each other, and a loud cry came out of my spirit –

I HAVE FORGOTTEN!!!!

I could feel the cry coming out of my body...out of my spirit!

It felt like the angels and heavenly hosts were trying to get me to remember who I am...who I was...before.

I stayed on the horse for a moment, getting used to the feel of her.

She knew me intimately.

I could tell because she allowed me to do all of this without bucking or moving or getting irritated.

We were comfortable together.

I felt that she missed me... (oh my, I could just cry right now).

I was trying to remember how to ride, but I couldn't remember.

I asked for a brush to brush her mane.

I started doing this, but an angel took the brush away from me and said that it was a distraction.

They were all adamant that I sit there on her back and remember – This is who I am!

Me and my horse!!

So, I sat there a while getting the feel of her.

I went to search, is this a female or male, her or him.

I tried to make it a him...but it was a HER!!...

A female ...

I asked her name - I searched, thinking, for her name...

HER NAME IS WISDOM!!!

And she is my horse, and I ride her, and we are intimate friends and companions!

I sat there a while just resting in all of this, getting TOTALLY blown away!!!!

It was overwhelming.

In the natural, I get up to go to the bathroom ... and I have a DEEP KNOWING ..that the Spirit of Wisdom that I had met a long while ago at a conference, who had been engaging me, teaching me lately – SHE IS MY HORSE!!

And I ride her, and I know her intimately!!!

A little while later, I asked Holy Spirit to show me what was before... who I was before ... and I saw myself mounting my horse, Wisdom, with one jump, landing with confidence on her back.

She has a crown upon her head, and I have a scroll in my right arm, and we ride forward. She kicks her front legs up and we ride forward!

Encounter at the Portal
with horses

3-8-2015

I wanted to give a testimony about what happened two Sunday nights ago at The Portal, a large house church that meets every Sunday night.

At the end of the evening, things started to get crazy.

A girl who we had ministered to greatly had been weeping most of the night and broke into Holy laughter so much so that it ignited the whole room. The drums started pounding a beat and the whole room erupted into this crazy, laughing, dancing, chaotic, trance-like atmosphere.

I was sitting in a fluffy, comfy chair. I was quiet, even amongst all the chaos. I felt the Lord pull me into the chair, almost as if I was disappearing into it.

Jesus came for me, and we ran up a staircase through a door and we ended up on the dance floor and danced for a long time.

We then mounted our horses. We were galloping hard and fast, not having anywhere to go, but just enjoying the fast pace of the gallop. We were going so fast!

Running running running...

At one point, we came to a hallway.

I saw Jesus take my past and put it behind a door and lock it, as if protecting me from it.

He stood in front of the door with His hands out like ... do not go in there.

I won't let you return to your past.

Then we were back on our horses...

Running, running running...

It was fun... I was joyful ...galloping hard and fast!!

We slowed down and my horse started to grow in stature, like Alice in Wonderland. She became huge! She became like a show horse adorned with armor.

I was riding her and could feel the nobility.

I watched as her legs were adorned with these beautiful armor-like shields that wrapped around her legs. She was so proud ...dancing and showing them off. Dancing like a show horse...side to side and prancing.

In the natural, back on earth in the room, I had people coming up to me, praying for me, not understanding where I was and praying, thinking I was having a hard time.

I was frozen in a trance and couldn't tell them that I was in an encounter with Jesus and that I was ok ... and to leave me alone.

I didn't want to come out of where I was, and people were pulling on me wanting me to speak to them.

It was funny because I could feel and see them trying to get me into the laughter and what was happening in the room, but I was somewhere else ... gone with Jesus, riding our horses together.

I had one girl recognize what was going on with me and she grabbed my hand and held it tight for an hour, like give me some of that!

I saw her get shot out into the heavens.

She started crying out, feeling the intensity of what was going on.

Then she started riding with me in my encounter.

She entered my encounter!

In the spirit, I threw her up on her horse and she understood how to ride. We rode together for a long while.

Then a guy came and sat down in front of me wanting me to pray for him.

All I could do was grab his hand.

I couldn't say anything...it was too good what was happening. I wanted to stay right where I was, in the encounter.

So, I have this girl on my right hand groaning from the encounter ... and this guy in front of me seeking His face ... drums all around and everyone in the room on the floor laughing and going crazy.

In the spirit, I invited the guy into my encounter.

I pushed him up on a horse, but he kept falling off. He didn't know how to ride.

I kept trying to show him how to ride, pushing him up on the horse, but he didn't know how.

When we were finished, I told him that God was going to teach him how to ride.

The whole time I was riding hard with Jesus, it was exhilarating.

We were riding hard like in the old western movies, we were riding across ...well... it wasn't the land... we were out in space, in the galaxies.

I could see stars all around and could feel the weightlessness of space around me.

Everything was so easy. I am not sure what we were riding across and why we were riding so hard.

I didn't stop to ask.

Sharing Stories at the Portal

10-18-2015

I shared some of my stories, my testimonies of my encounters, at the Portal last Sunday night and it was crazy wild.

I don't think I have ever shared with such supernatural power before!!

Kathie Walters had come for a visit and had a massive impact on me when she pulled the knife of accusation out of my back.

Here is that testimony:

When Kathy pulled that big knife of accusation out of my back, as well as a Jezebel knife, it was huge, like a hatchet, and I hit the floor under the Lord's anointing.

I could feel stuff oozing out of my back, years of accusations going back to the biggest ones that occurred while I was in France and all the way up until this moment.

I felt a flushing of tears, being washed cleaned.

Holy Spirit urging me to 'let it all out'.

I tried to stand up, but was so lightheaded that my head hit the ground again.

My friend was trying to help me, but I couldn't stand up.

I couldn't get my head off the floor.

I could feel my brain being rewired.

It felt like the top of my head was open and my brain was spilled out all over the floor.

I was aware of what was going on in the room, but my head was glued to the floor.

After much weeping, an angel came to minister to me.

It was a nurse-type angel. He had a first aid kit and knelt beside me and started to repair the huge gaping wound in my back.

I could feel his hand moving ever so slightly back and forth over the wound, creating a healing balm and growing skin back where it was open.

It took a while for that to happen.

So, I just lay there and let him finish. He was nice and gentle. It felt good and I knew it needed to happen.

Kathy came back while I was still on the floor and prayed against Freemasonry.

Then she came by again and said, 'You are a teacher and another word for teacher is Storyteller'.

I knew that was true and I knew I could do that, and it would be easy.

It witnessed so strongly in my spirit.

I knew I was to move on it.

(This was two years before I would get a job miraculously as a middle school teacher.)

After a while, I was able to get up. I didn't want to, but it was time, and I could.

The next day, I was different. I felt different. Lighter. No hatchets or knives in me.

The Lord had been guiding me forward to start sharing my encounters. I have had many encounters and I realized that I have never really shared them because of the accusation that was on them... and now it is gone!!

I told Kathie that I was going to share at the Portal, and she said, 'Start with the knife of accusation story and there will be deliverance'.

I took that as a word and knew it was going to be true.

It was interesting because as I was preparing to share the week before, Holy Spirit wouldn't let me prepare, wouldn't let me even think about what I was going to say or even start with.

Even that night, as I grabbed the microphone, I wasn't even sure what I was going to say, but I trusted Holy Spirit enough to lead me.

So, I did like she said, and I shared her word of what was going to happen.

I started telling my stories.

It felt like I was all over the place, but people told me afterward that it flowed all together and was powerful and it fit together well.

I asked at the end, when I finished speaking for people to come up if they felt led, for the knives of accusation to come out of their bodies.

Many in the room came up. In fact, most of the room came forward.

I wasn't sure what to do, so I just stood in front of each one and waited.

The first person, I pulled the knife of accusation out of their back, and they fell forward, weeping.

It happened again and again!

Most hit the floor, got lighter, changed color, got delivered.

It was a crazy night!

People are all over the floor!

It was so easy because I wasn't doing anything!

It was all Holy Spirit, and you could feel it... they could feel it!

I would just stand in front of people, and they would start weeping ... it was incredible!

Sometimes I would just stand there, and I could feel the Glory of God bursting out of me touching them and they would start to manifest and weep, feeling the powerful anointing coming all over them.

It was amazing for me to watch. I couldn't believe what was happening. It was all so easy.

I wanted to thank Kathie so much for whatever she imparted to me!

... or took out of me, so that things could flow... whatever it was ... thank you!

The river is flowing mightily in my life right now!!

She is one awesome lady!

Activation encounter
4-13-2015

I was just doing an activation with a minister online.

It was a visualization of opening the eyes of your heart and I went into an encounter:

1st encounter:

I imagined this big ancient doorway.

IT WAS HUGE.

I was little, like an ant.

The doorway was a mile high. This was not a doorway like I had ever seen before, like in my other encounters with the door of Revelation 3:20.

It was an old ancient door.

It was very inviting.

It opened before me.

I went through it very easily.

I didn't have to push it or anything.

When I went through the doorway, I could suddenly feel Jesus' presence very close – close to my face, as close as my breath. I could feel His beard on my cheek.

While this was happening, I could feel it in the natural.

I could feel the prickliness of it, and I couldn't move.

It was so intense.

I started to weep.

I felt like I was in the book of Song of Solomon, experiencing His intimate 'lover' love, like I was actually 'in the book'.

I could see the letters and words of the book floating around me.

I became her in the story. The one searching for her lover and finding him.

Jesus looked at me and lifted my head up by my chin and put His forehead on mine.

We stayed there for a while.

I could feel a ferocious love coming from Him, as I poured my hopelessness into Him.

He just kept looking at me. I could feel His eyes saturating my body.

All of this, I could feel in the natural...

On earth as it is in heaven.

2ⁿᵈ **encounter:**

Activation – spirit building word 4-14-2015

I entered into the activation and was immediately taken into yesterday's encounter, where I felt Jesus' beard on my cheek.

The intensity was greater this time. This was all felt in the natural too.

I felt His hand come behind my back and grab my other arm and take me on to the dance floor.

This was in 1ˢᵗ person – like I was actually <u>There</u>!

Normally, when I have been on the dance floor, I have been watching Him take me there, as if looking at it from afar, but this time <u>HE ACTUALLY TOOK ME</u>!

I could feel Him moving me, swaying me to and fro, and I felt again like I was living inside the book of Song of Solomon.

My body in the natural was moving to His leading.

It was so passionate.

I could feel His beard on my cheek as He moved me all over the dance floor.

Then I felt Him step back and take out a HUGE key.

Suddenly, on my chest appeared a keyhole and Jesus put the key in the keyhole in my chest.

I heard Him turn the key and then I heard a 'click' sound when He did that.

I thought, 'Oh, He is unlocking my heart! '

... I heard Him say... 'A garden enclosed He unlocks.'

He unlocked my secret garden.

In the Song of Solomon, it says, 'I am a garden enclosed, a locked garden', and He unlocked my garden.

(I had a HUGE confirmation of this the next day. A friend came to my house to give me a birthday present, and the Lord had told her I was His garden and she brought me 2 plants and a card with verses about I am His garden and verses from Song of Solomon!)

As He was unlocking my garden, I felt led to rent my chest.

I grabbed a hold of my clothes in the natural and made a gesture to rip them open and all this spiritual stuff came flying out of my chest.

My BIG diamond was still there in the middle of my chest, but what was coming out were ribbons and confetti, like a birthday party, bursting out of my chest.

Then I heard the minister leading the activation (I was still in his activation, but not following him at all) ... I heard him say, 'You can either stay here in this encounter or you can move on' ...

... and he took us in the activation to a hill where Jesus was teaching His disciples.

He said, 'Sit down.'

So, I did.

He said, 'Ask Jesus something.'

So, I did.

I asked Jesus about why this traumatic thing had happened to me in Tacoma when I was 20 something.

I was weeping deeply now.

He said... 'You were out of control, and I needed to stabilize you.'

Then I asked why my parents hadn't raised me the way they should've and why things had been so hard.

He said, 'They did – but you were out of control, making your own choices, going your own way. I needed to stabilize you – to ground you.'

Then I felt Jesus lift all my heavy burdens off my shoulders.

I suddenly saw shackles on my wrists and ankles. I did not know they were there, and I looked to make sure I wasn't making this up.

Yes...they were there.

I saw Jesus come and break the shackles off from my wrists and ankles. These were the constraints from the past that were on me to control me. I had let this come on me. I had come into agreement with the control.

Jesus broke them off!!

I wrote down:

I AM FREE!

FREE TO TRAVEL!!

FREE TO DO WHAT HE WANTS ME TO!!!_

Morning encounter
May 2nd @ 6am

After yesterday's meeting with the Northwest team of people bringing a Teacher from the UK here to the Pacific Northwest and then going to the Court of Kings and writing our own mandate, I woke up and wanted to do it again.

I asked Father to take me into the Court of the Kings.

As I entered, I noticed I was clothed in regal garments: my robe with signs and wonders following me was over my shoulders and running down my back and onto the floor. My crown was in place, and I had my scepter in my right hand.

I was greeted affectionately by everyone.

There were many Kings and they stood up as I came into the 'room'.

They all came up to me, excited that I was with them again.

One King, in particular, addressed me, saying that he was glad that I had come back.

He told me to stand up, to not kneel, as we were ALL Kings.

So, I stood up.

He took my hand regally and helped me up.

I said, 'I want to write a mandate. What should we write on it?'

I could feel such childlike joy in my whole being, like this play time was fun!!

I felt an idea come to me: write a mandate for this coming Sunday night's worship at the Portal.

Here is what I put on the mandate:

1.   That a new sound would be released that had never been heard before and the frequency and vibration of that new sound would resonate everything around it with the Glory of God.

2.   The sound would resonate in Vancouver and go out into the State and Nation

3.   That it WOULD BE HEARD AND FELT

There were other numerous things involving my destiny fulfillment, establishing of the sound, bringing people from far and wide.

All the Kings were aiding me in the writing of this mandate.

We were doing it together.

When we finished writing it together, I felt the scroll roll into my hand.

A King came forward and took it out of my hand and flung it out into space.... Far far far out into space.

I could see it go out and fly out into space, like it was going to accomplish something, and I knew it was a good thing.

That this was something that I was going to learn how to do, but didn't even know what it was doing at that moment.

This King then said he was Melchizedek!

He was different than the other Kings, seemed to be other than.

I wasn't sure where we were at that moment.

We didn't seem to be in the Court of Kings anymore, almost like we were outside of time and space.

He was full of everything: wisdom, knowledge, understanding.

You could feel it.

It embodied him and I trusted him immediately.

He was dressed like a professor when they are dressed in their garments, with the robes and all the tassels and mantles around their necks.

He was kind and gentle and had a beard.

I was a little worried about the scroll going out into space and not having gone into the other courts and the protocol of all that.

He felt me think that and he took me quickly through the Court of the Chancellors, the Scribes and the Angels with the scroll, completing the protocol as I 'knew' them.

He told me that mature Sons don't need to do all of that. These things were training wheels to help in the process of understanding and that I had graduated and didn't need to do those protocols anymore.

Melchizedek then took me on a walk with him.

Walking alongside him, he started to tell me some things about myself. He was very loving, concerned about me. He knew me and all about my life.

He said many things to me.

One big thing I remember that sticks out is that he told me about how he had held back the darkness and the enemy now for 15 years that had wanted to come and destroy me, kill me, annihilate me.

I remembered the scripture in Daniel 10:12-14, where it says how Michael had restrained the prince of Persia for 21 days and I felt the power of what he had done for me in the restraining.

This darkness that had come against me had brought great testing and trials and Melchizedek showed me how I had held steadfast.

He was pleased at how I had held onto Jesus so tight.

I told him that I had no choice, that He was my breath.

Melchizedek said that I had had a choice and I had chosen rightly.

I then saw him stamp the word STEADFAST on me, into my skin, like I had passed a test or season or something and that was my 'certificate' and I was moving on.

He said, now that is all over. This is a new time, a new day for you, and all that you have struggled in and for will now become easy.

As you decree and declare out of your mouth, it will be so.

... and right at that moment, the neighbor's irritating dog started to bark... and I said – you will be quiet, and I put my finger (in the spirit) over the dog's mouth, silencing it.

The minute I did that... THE DOG STOPPED BARKING!

It was a Miracle!!!!

And I knew that what Melchizedek had said was true.

Melchizedek then showed me how to be a King.

He said – Go on, start declaring what you want.

The minute he said that a brand-new scepter came into my right hand, replacing my old one.

This new scepter was larger and had several round swirling balls of galaxies swirling around in them stacked on top of each other at the top of it.

It fit my hand rightly.

So, I did. I started to put forth my hands and my new scepter.

As I raised my hands, I could feel the difference in the power in the DNA of my words increase and magnify.

AS A KING DECREES – SO IT IS!

Melchizedek was showing me the level of increase that had been unlocked and released to me. I started to decree some things over my neighbors and cracked open some things in my neighborhood and city, just trying it out, like test driving a new car.

We walked along together for some time, like old friends, like a true father, mentor, but not really that.

It was so loving, nurturing, helping me to come into all that I am created to be and he has been there all along, fighting for me – holding back darkness – so it doesn't consume me.

All of that he showed me, and I knew it was true.

I suddenly remembered that he was in charge of the finances in heaven, and I asked him to release it.

He showed me how to take my scepter and crack the ground and open up the ancient wells of provision.

So, I did.

We walked for some time, talking and conversing. It seemed as if we were in a meadow. There was green grass everywhere.

At one point, a bridge made of grass and cobblestones opened up and Melchizidek guided me towards the bridge.

It felt ancient, like something from a long time ago.

As we were crossing the bridge together, Joan of Arc appeared, coming towards us from the other side of the bridge.

The honor bestowed in the moment was felt.

I wasn't sure what to do, so I curtsied in respect of the visit.

There were no words spoken, but we were communicating heart to heart.

She asked me to kneel, and I did.

She had a large sword in her hand, and it was engraved with words and symbols that were not clear to me, but they felt significant.

She proceeded to take her sword and rested on each of my shoulders, knighting me.

Melchizidek seemed pleased.

The moment felt intense and weighted with significance that I was not sure what was going on or what it meant, but I knew in my spirit that this was a defining moment for me.

.... And then I fell back asleep.

5/17/2015
In private time with the Lord

From my activation journal:

Jesus met me as I stepped into heaven, and He took my hand.

We walked down this narrow pathway in space and came to the war room.

I wanted the blueprint for my life.

A very nice man, a being, met me.

It felt like he had been waiting for me for a long time.

The room was like a gun shop, with weapons and achievements on the walls.

In the center of the room was a huge table with chairs around it.

I asked for my blueprint and said, 'It is going to be easier to work everything out if I have it.'

The man said that I couldn't have all of it.

They were all being secretive, looking at each other, like they knew what was on the blueprint.

I said, 'Well, give me what you can.'

He laid out a portion of it on the big table.

I said, 'Well, how do I work this out?'

He didn't answer.

I took the blueprint and scroll, and then Melchizidek showed up on my left side.

I felt he was there to help me.

I said, 'Let's take it into the Court of Kings and write out a mandate to outwork the blueprint.'

We went into the Court of Kings and asked for a mandate to legislate what was written on it.

... but when I went to write it – I couldn't write.

I thought that if I took out a mandate to legislate, that the Kings would help me write it.

Well, that didn't work out.

I asked Melchizidek, 'What do I do now?'

I was led to go on my mountain and start declaring that the stadium vision would be outworked, and all the promises of God would too.

As I was doing that, Melchizidek asked if I wanted to meet Joan of Arc.

Just before that moment, I was being shown who I am and I saw the vision of me on my horse, Wisdom, standing up in the straps of the saddle, shooting arrows into nations, unlocking them.

I started to weep because of my heritage in France.

He took me to meet her. We embraced. She knighted me and told me Melchizidek was one of the voices she had heard.

She knighted me for battle and said I was ready.

I saw how I was going to lead the troops like she did. I felt this so deep in my spirit, I was crying.

The whole time I was in this encounter, I was feeling that everyone knew something about me that I didn't and they were all being secretive, not wanting to unveil too much too soon.

They were handling me with care.

We embraced and I left her and traveled down that narrow pathway.

I still had my portion of my blueprint, my scroll, and I took it into the Court of the Chancellors.

They stamped it with the Yod Hey Vav Hey* key stamp.

One of the Chancellors came up to me, put his hand on my shoulders and said, 'We are all very proud of you.'

I felt he was happy I was there doing what I was doing.

I took the blueprint into the Court of the Scribes.

As I walked in, I could see my Kingly attire: my robe, my crown, my scepter – nobility.

I came in and greeted them and thanked them for making a record of it.

I came into the Court of the Angels and a whole bunch of angels greeted me, laughing, delighted.

I opened my hand, and they eagerly took their part of the assignment and I released them.

Then I felt the Lord pulling me to Him.

I was looking at Jesus and thanking Him and was pulled into the face of God.

I said, 'I love you.'

He said, 'I love you more.'

I felt the intense weight of love go through me, into me, and I was overcome.

The Lord said, 'You have been so faithful, through the testing and the trials. I trust you. You are faithful. I trust you.'

He showed me where testing had come and I had stood firm in His grip, following His every lead.

He took me up above the atmosphere and I saw three dragons – fear, inadequacy, and insecurity.

I felt led to slay them.

I took my sword and for each one – I cut their head off – then the tail – and slit its belly and gouged out all that was inside.

I saw it flow out into the city and region.

The Lord said that was for me.

Then I heard Him say, 'I am going to put my hand on your body.'

I saw this huge hand hover over my body.

It was as big as my body!

As it started to press into me, calling my body into alignment with Him, I saw these things, these beings, cry out and leave the sides of me.

Wow!

I went back on my mountain and declared my house will serve the Lord.

I took my scepter and lifted the veil off of everyone.

I could see them standing up, facing a direction, arms out, eyes closed, looking up – but a veil was over each one of them.

I took my scepter and lifted off the veil.

*Footnote - Yod Hey Vav Hey – YHWH – Yahweh - the Hebrew word for God

Testimony – Cle Elum retreat - July 19-23, 2015

There were 72 participants.

That is important.

We did a class action mobile court case dealing with the false trinity and the false 7 spirits of God.

It was powerful.

We did it in the afternoon session.

I left the session after the collective mobile court case with this 'sleepy I have to go take a nap right now' kind of feeling.

My body had this sense of extreme rest, calm and peace come over it.

Whatever had been driving me was gone and everything felt condensed down.

I could feel it in my body, that feeling of deep rest.

I kept seeing, in my mind's eye, an elevator going down in an elevator shaft, that feeling when you get to the bottom.

I'm having trouble explaining this feeling with words.

I wasn't sure what to think about what had just happened.

I was weirded out a little.

I went to my room and took a long, luxurious nap.

Come the evening session during worship, I came to the front, closed my eyes and wasn't expecting anything to be different, but it was.

Everything was different.

Instead of my usual seeing and easily entering heaven, I had blackness... nothing. Black screen on my eyelids.

This wasn't the black cloud. I have been there twice now.

This was nothing, like a slate wiped clean, like let's start over, shall we?

I was standing there in worship for a while, and I started to hear the chatter in my mind, in my consciousness of ... 'what have you done?' ... 'you've done something wrong' ... 'oh no, you have to go back and undo this' ... 'this is all wrong' ... 'this is the devil'.

I started to look, to observe, what was being said in my mind and I felt a familiar pull to go down that pathway of those words, but I knew that wasn't right and pushed it aside.

I told the thoughts to stop and go away ... and they went.

I pushed all that aside and waited for a moment.

After a little while I said, 'Father?'... 'Abba?'

I waited for a response, and I heard him say, 'I've got you, don't worry.'

It felt to me as if He was holding things back from me because the rush of information of what had just happened would be too overwhelming for me to handle all at once.

One thing I am confident about is His ability to lead me rightly. I trust His hand on me and His leadership.

So, I just stayed that way during worship.

I was having a very hard time and it all felt weird.

Different.

The evening session passed. It was great.

I got to my room that night and got into bed and said, 'Father, I untether my spirit'.

The minute I closed my eyes, I saw in the spirit like it was on TV.

I normally see on my black screen, when I close my eyes, images and pictures, but not in color, sometimes a little bit of color, but dimly.

But this time, the pictures were moving and in bright color, like I was seeing things happen right then, like peering into lives and seeing what was happening in real time.

Pictures rolled across in front of my eyes.

The first picture opened up and pulled me into the galaxies and flung me out.

Then the pictures kept coming until I fell asleep.

I could feel the adjustment in relating to the real Trinity and 7 spirits of God.

I could feel their love for me in holding things back to not totally overwhelm me, as I think I would disintegrate from the power of it, the weight was so strong.

I could feel this new strength in my body.

Where I had a revelation of Oneness with Him before, I was now the revelation.

I was what I believed.

I could feel the deeper revelation of Oneness in my body, like a rod, like iron strength. 'You cannot move me' kind of strength.

During the worship in the morning, I had my feet plugged into the floor. Something or someone had cemented my feet to the floor.

I couldn't move them, and I heard the Lord say, 'I am totally resequencing your DNA'.

I felt glued to the floor and felt liquid gold being poured into my body.

This is what I 'felt' after the court case.

I could feel its strength in my body!

I knew things were totally different now and I was a little weirded out. I knew this was going to take some time for things to unravel and unpack.

I felt assurance and peace that I had completely shut everything down in August and could rest in the timing of the Lord to reveal everything in His timing.

So, I get home, sleep an amazing first night's sleep.

I get up the next morning and go out to water my plants outside, and I could hear them communicating with me, all of them.

I have had experiences where I could hear the trees clapping for me as I walked by, but this was way different.

They were talking to me, conversing with me, telling me how much water to give them, to splash their leaves and how much.

One told me when I asked it, 'Does this hurt to spray your leaves like that?'

It responded, 'yes that hurts, point the water here'.

One bush was giggling and being tickled, delighting, and playing as the water was being sprayed on him.

I went to each one and they each spoke to me.

One was over in the back and kept saying, I'm so thirsty.

So, I went over and watered it until it told me to stop.

Now ... THAT IS DIFFERENT!

I am beginning to understand the magnitude and why Father held, is holding it back, and releasing it little by little.

Wow!

PART THREE

Activations

Introduction

Definition of an activation: the action or process of making active or operative

How do you activate something?

To activate something is to start it off, trigger it, set it in motion.

To activate something is to make it active.

We are asked to do things by faith.

These activations are activating our faith to call the unseen realm into the seen realm and make it manifest.

In other words, framing our world, creating with our breath and thoughts, and bringing those things, those desires, into being so that we can walk out our destinies.

Framing/Manifesting:

Inside of you resides the glory of God.

That resurrection power that raised Christ from the dead lives inside of you.

There is no separation.

No separating you from His presence.

He is in you, and you are in Him.

That glory that lives inside of you has creative power, a creative miracle power that can bring things from the unseen realm into the seen realm.

Meaning – you create your own destiny.

You create, you manifest, what is around you with your thoughts and your words. If you don't like what is happening to you and around you, just change your words. It will change the atmosphere around you. It will change things in your life and what is in front of you.

These activations are meant to accomplish just that.

When doing these activations, prepare yourself, get somewhere comfortable, where you will not be distracted.

Turn your phone and iPad off.

Try to be somewhere you will not be bothered.

It might be a good idea to have a pad and a pen to write revelations and other distractions down.

For each activation, take your time.

Make sure Holy Spirit is with you, guiding you, leading you.

With each step, stay there until you are led to go onto the next step.

Don't rush this.

The Lord has things He wants to reveal to you, major things for your destiny.

Prepare your heart and mind, be open and receive.

I would read through the activation to see where you are going and then close your eyes and enter in and follow what is written and if Holy Spirit takes you on a different pathway, that is ok too.

Go where He leads.

After each activation, stay there as long as you feel Holy Spirit wants you to be there.

He will lead you rightly.

He might have you go to other places, like your secret garden and bury your encounter there; or on top of your mountain and make declarations; or release documents to the angels to accomplish.

Just remember - take your time and don't rush things.

Let's go.

Activation #1
The Door to other realms

Get somewhere comfortable where you will not be distracted.

Turn your phone and iPad off.

Try to be somewhere you will not be bothered.

It might be a good idea to have a pad and a pen to write revelations and things down.

Remember to take your time and be led by Holy Spirit to each phase.

Don't leave until you feel a release to move on.

Let's go.

You can close your eyes or not.

I like to close my eyes.

It helps with seeing.

Fix your eyes on Yeshua.

Feel His rest and peace.

His shalom.

(It might take a minute to calm down, calm your mind and body down.)

Feel heavens open invitation to come into His presence.

Yeshua is the gate.

The door.

He is there waiting for you.

John 10:9 – I am the gate; whoever enters through me will be saved.

Imagine His outstretched hand.

Take His outstretched hand and walk through the gateway, the doorway.

Let Him take you through the dimensions of heaven.

Ask Yeshua to take you through the Kingdom of God to the Kingdom of Heaven.

Ask Yeshua to take you onto your mountain and to show you what is there.

(Your mountain is your life).

Here there are thrones and scepters and mantles.

Activate your angels and ask what their names are.

Ask Yeshua to give you your mantle of Authority.

Ask for your scepter, which is the authority to rule.

Ask for your crown to be placed on your head – He crowns you with glory and honor.

Ask for your scroll to be delivered to you, which is the blueprint for your life.

Let Him unfurl your scroll.

Let Him unravel your scroll, your longings, and desires.

Soak in the revelation that is written on your scroll.

Remember - You wrote your scroll with Him, in agreement, before the foundations were created.

Remember – remember ..

This activation can be done many times. You can enter it as many times as you need to to feel it is complete.

It might not happen all at once. You might have to go back into the encounter to receive all that He has for you.

Be patient.

Everything is in His timing.

Everything is working for your good.

Activation #2
The Doorway to heaven

Revelation 3:20

Get somewhere comfortable where you will not be distracted.

Turn your phone and iPad off.

Try to be somewhere you will not be bothered.

It might be a good idea to have a pad and pen to write revelations and things down.

Remember to take your time and be led by Holy Spirit to each phase.

Don't leave until you feel a release to move on.

Let's go.

Encounter with the doorway of heaven

Revelation 3:20

Here I am! I stand at the door and knock. If anyone hears my voice and opens the door, I will come in and eat with that person, and they with me.

Close your eyes.

Open the eyes of your heart.

Deep breath. Selah.

Imagine a doorway.

Picture the door in your spirit – Yeshua is knocking at that door.

Open the door, let Him in – the door handle is on your side.

You open it and let Him in.

Feel the LOVE, ACCEPTANCE and AFFIRMATION as He greets you.

Hear the sound, feel the vibration of Him.

He is affirming your identity.

He is affirming your calling.

He is affirming your destiny.

Listen to His voice.

Feel your heart engage with Him, with the atmosphere around Him.

Now ... Step through that door into heaven.

Yeshua takes you by the hand and leads you through the atmospheres of heaven.

The Presence of God is manifesting.

He takes you to the place where you are seated in heaven at His right hand.

Open your heart even further.

Let Him lead you to YOD HEY SHIN VAV HEY

This is where you sit in the middle of His name, where all authority and power come from.

I would encourage you to stay right here and let Holy Spirit reveal truth to your heart.

Take your time.

Breathe.

Activation #3
Book of Remembrance

Get somewhere comfortable where you will not be distracted.

Turn your phone and iPad off.

Try to be somewhere you will not be bothered.

It might be a good idea to have a pad and a pen to write revelations and things down.

Remember to take your time and be led by Holy Spirit to each phase.

Don't leave until you feel a release to move on.

Let's go.

Write a Book of Remembrance ...

Close your eyes and go to that place where you are seated with Him in heavenly places in the middle of His name – YOD HEY SHIN VAV HEY (from activation #2)

Ask the Lord to open up your timeline.

(Wait for that to unfold.)

See your timeline stretch out in front of you, from beginning to end. From the beginning of your life to right now and to the end.

See it stretch out into the horizon.

Ask Holy Spirit to come and help you see it.

Ask Him to reveal to you each year of your life.

Take your time.

Outline each year of your life.

Take each year one by one and write down what Holy Spirit is revealing to you.

Some years will have more than others. This is ok.

This will take some time. It might take days, weeks, maybe months, but it is worth it.

(When I did this, I had already written down on a big piece of paper the year from the time of my birth up until the present year in my life. Each year written down in the margin of a piece of paper. I had done this on a big sheet of paper and left space to fill in and write as He led me.)

Activation #4
Opening up your ancient doors

Get somewhere comfortable where you will not be distracted.

Turn your phone and iPad off.

Try to be somewhere you will not be bothered.

It might be a good idea to have a pad and a pen to write revelations and things down.

Remember to take your time and be led by Holy Spirit to each phase.

Don't leave until you feel a release to move on.

Let's go.

Opening up your ancient doors of your inheritance and provision

Close your eyes and go to that place where you are seated with Him in heavenly places in the middle of His name – YOD HEY SHIN VAV HEY (from activation #2)

This activation is more of an asking and waiting.

The Lord has made provision for you and your destiny and calling.

Sit and ask Him to open up YOUR ancient doors of provision for you.

Activation #5
Declarations over your life

Get somewhere comfortable where you will not be distracted.

Turn your phone and iPad off.

Try to be somewhere you will not be bothered.

It might be a good idea to have a pad and a pen to write revelations and things down.

Remember to take your time and be led by Holy Spirit to each phase.

Don't leave until you feel a release to move on.

Let's go.

Make Declarations over your Life.

Close your eyes and go to that place where you are seated with Him in heavenly places in the middle of His name – YOD HEY SHIN VAV HEY (from activation #2)

Go on top of your mountain and declare:

I am a child of the Living God.

I am an heir of God and a joint heir with Jesus Christ.

I am a new creation in Jesus and old things have passed away and all things have become new.

I am chosen.

I am a Co-Creator with God.

I am a King and Priest unto my God.

The law of the Spirit of Life in Christ Jesus has set me free from the laws of sin and death.

I am cleansed by Yeshua' blood.

I am an overcomer because of Yeshua' blood and because of the word of my testimony.

No weapon formed against me shall prosper.

I have the mind of Christ.

Greater is He that is in me than he that is in the world.

I am ONE with Him.

Nothing can separate us.

I am the righteousness of God in Jesus.

I am free.

I am the head not the tail.

I am seated with Christ in heavenly places, far above principalities and powers.

I am seated in the middle of His name ... in the middle of Yod Hey Vav Hey.

I am assured that all things work together for my good.

I Have been established, anointed, and sealed by God.

I am a citizen of heaven.

I am the salt and the light of the earth.

I am a branch of the true vine.

I can do all things through Christ who strengthens me.

Activation #6
Know God more

Get somewhere comfortable where you will not be distracted.

Turn your phone and iPad off.

Try to be somewhere you will not be bothered.

It might be a good idea to have a pad and pen to write revelations and things down.

Remember to take your time and be led by Holy Spirit to each phase.

Don't leave until you feel a release to move on.

Let's go.

Press delete on what you know of God to experience more.

Get in a quiet spot.

Engage heaven and the place where you are seated in heavenly places in the middle of His name.

Imagine the Sea of Glass in front of you.

Take the crown off of your head.

Take your crowns ... this is your life, your encounters and your experiences and everything that you think you know of God.

... and lay it down on the Sea of Glass, as an offering ... a love offering... offering back to Him what He gave you.

Tell the Lord:

Lord, I press delete on all that I know of you, so that I can experience and encounter you more.

I want to know you more.

Activation #7
Meditate on Jesus

Get somewhere comfortable where you will not be distracted.

Turn your phone and iPad off.

Try to be somewhere you will not be bothered.

It might be a good idea to have a pad and a pen to write revelations and things down.

Remember to take your time and be led by Holy Spirit to each phase.

Don't leave until you feel a release to move on.

Let's go.

Focus on Jesus ... Meditate on Him.

Jesus

He is the first and last, the beginning and the end.

He is the keeper of Creation and the creator of all.

He is the Architect of the universe and the manager of all times.

He always was, He always is, and He always will be.

Unmoved, Unchanged, Undefeated, and never Undone.

He was bruised and brought healing.

He was pierced and eased pain.

He was persecuted and brought freedom.

He was dead and brought life.

He is risen and brings power.

He reigns and brings peace.

He is light, love, longevity, and Lord.

He is goodness, kindness, gentleness, and God.

He is Holy, righteous, mighty, powerful, and pure.

His word is eternal.

His will is unchanging.

His mind is on me.

He is my Redeemer.

He is my Savior.

He is my guide.

He is my peace.

He is my joy.

He is my comfort.

He is my Lord.

His bond is love.

His burden is light.

He is the wisdom of the wise.

The power of the powerful.

The Ancient of Days.

The Ruler of rulers.

The Leader of leaders.

The Sovereign Lord of all that was and is and is to come.

He will never leave me.

He will never forsake me.

He will never mislead me.

He will never forget me.

He will never overlook me.

He lifts me up.

He is strong.

He is the way.

He is my courage.

He steadies me.

He heals me.

He leads me.

He shields me.

He comforts me.

He provides for me.

He is everything.

He is God.

He is faithful

I am His

He is mine.

Activation #8
Jesus His thoughts about you

Get somewhere comfortable where you will not be distracted.

Turn your phone and iPad off.

Try to be somewhere you will not be bothered.

It might be a good idea to have a pad and a pen to write revelations and things down.

Remember to take your time and be led by Holy Spirit to each phase.

Don't leave until you feel a release to move on.

Let's go.

Focus on Jesus and have Him come and speak to you.

Get a pen and paper and be ready to write down what He says.

Invite Jesus to come.

Ask Him what He thinks of you.

Ask Him how He sees you.

Ask Him what is on His mind.

.. and wait....

Start writing when He starts to talk to you and reveal His thoughts to you.

Activation #9
Mobile court protocol

Get somewhere comfortable where you will not be distracted.

Turn your phone and iPad off.

Try to be somewhere you will not be bothered.

It might be a good idea to have a pad and a pen to write revelations and things down.

Remember to take your time and be led by Holy Spirit to each phase.

Don't leave until you feel a release to move on.

Let's go.

Understanding the mobile courts of heaven

Protocols of the mobile courts of heaven

Background- here are some scriptures to lay a foundation for you about the courts of heaven.

Justice and courtroom are words you can find throughout the word of God. His heart is for righteousness and justice. They are the foundations of His throne.

Both Daniel and John saw a time where we, the saints, would be given justice in the courts of heaven.

One amazing thing is that it is all rigged in our favor.

We win!

Yahweh, our Father is the judge.

Yeshua is our mediator.

Holy Spirit is the orchestrator of all of it and brings truth to light.

The word of God is our Bill of Rights and every promise we have from Him is Yes! And amen!

Revelation 3:20 ... Behold, I stand at the door and knock ... Come up here.

Court: a place in the heavenly realm where Kingdom judgment and justice are administered.

One goes to the courts of heaven with authority.

Revelation 4:1-5 ... 1 *after these things, I saw a door standing open in heaven. The first voice that I had heard speaking to me like a trumpet said, 'Come up here, and I will show you what must happen after this.' 2 Instantly, I was in the Spirit, and I saw a throne in heaven with a person seated on a throne. 3 The person sitting there looked like jasper and carnelian, and there was a rainbow around the throne that looked like an emerald. 4 Around the throne were 24 other thrones, and on these thrones sat 24 elders wearing white robes and gold victor's crowns on their heads. 5 Flashes of lightning, noises, and peals of thunder came from the throne. Burning in front of the throne were seven flaming torches, which are the seven spirits of God.*

Zechariah 3:1-6 ... 1 *Then the messenger angel showed me Joshua, the High Priest, standing in the presence of the angel of the Lord, and standing at his right to accuse him 2 And the Lord said to satan, 'The Lord rebuke you, O satan! The Lord who has chosen Jerusalem rebukes you! This man is a burning brand plucked from the fire, is he not?'*

3 Now Joshua was standing before the angel, clothed with filthy garments. 4 And the angel said to those who were standing before him, 'Remove the filthy garments from him.' And to him he said, 'Behold I have taken your sin away from you, and I will clothe you in rich apparel.'

5 And I said, 'Let them put a clean turban on his head.' So, they put a clean turban on his head and clothed him with garments; and the angel of the Lord was standing by.

6 ... and the angel of the Lord admonished Joshua saying, 7 'thus says the Lord of Hosts, 'If you will walk in MY ways and if you will perform My laws, then you will also govern MY house and also have charge of MY courts, and I will grant you free access among these who are standing here.

These verses represent an example of the courtroom in heaven.

The Lord promised Joshua he would have access to the heavenly courts if he was obedient to God's ways. Joshua was in filthy clothes when he went in, but he was given new garments, which represent forgiveness and the washing away of our sins with Jesus' blood.

We go into court to get clean, delivered of our sin and the sins of our generations. And he was given a new turban, which represents the mind of Christ.

The promise is that, if we are obedient to His ways, we can govern and make decisions.

We are Kings and Priests unto our God, and we are going to participate in the government of heaven invading the earth.

*Daniel 7:9-10 ... 9 I kept on watching until the Ancient of Days was seated. His clothes were white, like snow, and the hair on His head was like pure wool. His throne burned with flaming fire, and its wheels burned with fire. 10 A river of fire flowed out from before him. Thousands upon thousands were serving Him, with millions upon millions waiting before Him. **The court sat in judgment, and the record books were unsealed.**

*Daniel 7:22 ... until the ancient of Days arrived to pass judgment in favor of the saints of the Highest One and the time came for the saints to take possession of the Kingdom.

*Isaiah 41:21-22 ... 'Put forward your case!' says the Lord. 'Submit your arguments!' says Jacob's King. Let them approach and ask us, 'what will happen?' As to the former things, what were they? Tell us, so that we may consider them and know. Or the latter things or the things to come – let us hear.

There are other scriptures to check out:

*Job 2:1-8

*Luke 22:31-34

*Revelation 12:10

Satan is asking for permission as an accuser to destroy and kill the saints in the courts every single time. It is where he gets his authority, because we have acted out in sin and there are legal documents where satan is able to act on.

More scripture on the courtroom in the bible:

<u>*Amos 5:15</u> ... Hate evil, love good, and establish justice in the courts*

<u>*Psalm 100:4</u> ... Enter His gates with thanksgiving and his courts with praise; give thanks to him and praise his name.*

<u>*Psalm 35</u> ... says, 'Plead my cause, O Lord, with them that strive with me, fight against them that fight against me.'*

<u>*Job 13:18</u> ... now I have prepared my case, I know that I will be vindicated.*

The mobile courts of heaven are where the enemy sits night and day and accuses.

I had heard about the mobile courts years ago and my curiosity led me into an encounter with Holy Spirit, who then taught me a protocol when engaging the mobile court.

I stepped in by faith and Holy Spirit led me so gently.

It was an amazing experience.

I had no idea what I was doing but He knew and led me into all truth.

The courtroom is a place of repentance for yourself, alone.

Before, when I used to lead worship, I would run for cover, afterwards hiding in the shadow of His wings. I had too much on my trading floor and the enemy would always hit me hard. The enemy had legal right to come after me.

If you are getting hit by the enemy, that means he has legal right to do that.

You need to clear your trading floor, deal with your stuff.

It will make a huge difference for you, clear the filters off of your sight and your hearing and your discernment will increase.

Repenting shuts the enemy's mouth!

Protocol For The Mobile Courts Of Heaven

1. Step into the place where you are seated in heavenly places, in the middle of His name – Yod Hey Shin Vav Hey

2. Activate the mobile courts of heaven – say – Father, I activate the mobile courts of heaven

3. Honor who is there – Honor Father, as judge. Honor Yeshua, as our great mediator. Honor Holy Spirit who orchestrates everything. Honor the great cloud of witnesses who show up. There might be others who show up, like the men in white linen or the angels and angelic canopy or Melchizedek or the fiery burning ones or the Heavenly Hosts .. honor them.

4. Repent – for the first time entering, I like to say – Father, I repent for my sins and the sins of my generations and then follow Holy Spirit where He leads you to repent.

Stay here as long as you need to or as long as you can. You can always come back. This is not a one and done.

(I spent 9 months in the mobile courts when I first started, going in sometime 4-5 times a day the first 3 months, peeling away at the onion. Now, I go in when Holy Spirit leads.)

5. When you are finished repenting ...

6. Judgment comes ... remember ... we win!!

Ask the Lord to judge you according to His covering, which is the blood of Yeshua of Nazareth, which washes away all sin.

7. Ask for the legal documents/the papers of freedom – hold out your hands during this part, as the documents will be delivered to you.

These are documents of your freedom from accusation from what you have repented of.

My first time, I held my hands out and there were so many documents that there was a heavenly forklift delivering my documents to me. It took a while ... so wait until they are all delivered.

8. From here, there are several things that you can do.

I used to have the papers burned up. Then, I used to bury them in my secret garden. I used to put them into my mountain.

But now, after Melchizedek taught me, I take them all and I throw them out into the atmosphere, commanding the angels to deliver them to whoever needs to have them and be notified of my freedom from torment.

9. Make sure as you back out of the court that you are honoring.

Remember that this is all Holy Spirit led.

Let the Spirit of truth lead you in this.

This protocol is a skeleton to follow, but be led by Holy Spirit.

Special Acknowledgements

This book is a testament to perseverance, divine intervention, and the kindness of friends. I'm deeply grateful to two special people who were instrumental in bringing this project to life.

To my dear friend, **Jenny Pizot**, you have been my biggest cheerleader since I started this journey in 2019. Your unwavering support, constant encouragement, and gentle nudges kept me going when I wanted to quit. Thank you for never letting me forget the book I was meant to finish.

To another cherished friend, **Lucy Escobar**, thank you for being a divinely aligned partner in this process. When I finally found the courage to prepare the manuscript, you were there every step of the way, offering practical help and support. You were a crucial part of the initial push to get this ready.

Lastly, and most importantly, this book would still be a non-starter without the guidance of the **Holy Spirit**. I had reached a point of exhaustion with the self-publishing process and was ready to give up. The manuscript was complete, but the thought of all the tedious work that remained was too much. I had decided this book would never see the light of day.

Then, at the Joyfest conference last July, in the middle of a powerful session, the Holy Spirit shouted to me in my spirit: **PUBLISH YOUR BOOK NOW!** I wrestled with the thought, telling myself I was too tired and didn't have the skills to finish. But the Holy Spirit—Ruach HaKodesh—spoke straight to my heart, energizing me with the promise that Lucy would help.

I wrestled with Holy Spirit's instruction, exhausted and overwhelmed by the task ahead. But Holy Spirit revitalized my heart and gave me the strength to try again. Lucy was all in, and we worked together to prepare the manuscript. But as we neared the end of the self-publishing process, I hit another wall. The tedious, technical details felt impossible, and I felt helpless.

In that moment of wrestling, the Lord instructed me to join a Zoom meeting in the Creative Space community on Facebook where Chris Blackeby was speaking. To my astonishment, Chris spoke exclusively about publishing books. I sat there in my pajamas, listening, knowing in my heart that this was no coincidence. I immediately explored his website, Seraph Creative, and sent a message.

After two months of waiting, I was led to simply release the project to the universe, trusting that it would find its way to the right place and people.

The very next morning, an email landed in my inbox: they wanted to publish my book!

They took my manuscript and transformed it into this stunningly beautiful book you hold in your hands.

I am forever grateful for all of this and the ones who have nudged me, prodded me, wooed me, and encouraged me to finish.

Thank you from an eternally grateful heart.

About the author

Bracy Wevers is a multifaceted artist, a lightworker, and a called-out one, passionately ushering in a new era, dedicated to awakening potential. With her upcoming debut book, the culmination of years of passion and dedication, Bracy aims to encourage and inspire readers to embrace their innate power to dream, create and invent. As a musician, songwriter, recording artist, author, and painter, she draws on her unique ability to move in heavenly realms and trust her intuition, believing that every step of the journey serves a greater good.

For it is in the journey that we delight.

SeraphCreative

Heaven's Heart for Earth

Seraph Creative is a collective of artists, writers, theologians & illustrators who desire to see the body of Christ grow into full maturity, walking in their inheritance as Sons of God on the Earth.

Sign up to our newsletter to know about future exciting releases.

Visit our website: www.seraphcreative.org

www.ingramcontent.com/pod-product-compliance
Lightning Source LLC
Chambersburg PA
CBHW071720120626
46550CB00001B/314